Thinking Through
Activities from Biology 1

Hugh Graham   James Lewis   Maria Spencer

SERIES EDITOR: DAVID EDWARDS

UNWIN
HYMAN

Published in 1989 by
Unwin Hyman Limited
15–17 Broadwick Street
London W1V 1FP

© Hugh Graham, James Lewis, Maria Spencer 1989

All rights reserved. No part of this publication may be reproduced, stored in a retrieval system, or transmitted in any form or by any means, electronic, mechanical, photocopying, recording or otherwise, without the prior permission of Unwin Hyman Limited.

British Library Cataloguing in Publication Data

Graham, Hugh
   Activities from biology.—(Thinking through
Science)
Bk. 1
1. Biology
I. Title II. Spencer, Maria III. Lewis, James
IV. Series
574

ISBN 0-7135-2853-2

Typeset by MS Filmsetting Ltd, Frome
Origination by Chroma Graphics, Singapore
Printed and bound by New Interlitho, Italy

Cover photograph by Martyn Chillmaid
Book design by Juliet and Charles Snape

Contents

About this book (v)

Unit
1 The Good, the Bad and the Ugly 2
2 What Makes a Weed Successful? 4
3 Spotting the Difference 6
4 On the Beach 8
5 Super Human! 10
6 S-Factors 12
7 Having Children 14
8 The Right Choice 16
9 Mouth Matters 18
10 Confined to the Cell 20
11 Coronary Heart Disease 22
12 Aerobics 24
13 Grow Your Own 26
14 Unhappy Houseplants 28
15 Keep out the Killer 30
16 Goodies and Baddies 32
17 It's Just a Phase 34
18 Message on a Bottle 36
19 It's all in the Genes 38
20 A Tale of the River Bed 40

Content Matrix for the National Curriculum 42
Index 43
Acknowledgements 44

About this book

These exercises are about important applications of biology. Some of the information you will have to read—some of it you will have to get from the tables, charts and pictures. You will use this information and what you already know about biology to answer the questions.

Thinking Through Science, Biology 1 will help you to understand some useful biological ideas. But most of all, we hope that the book will let you enjoy biology—a very important part of our everyday lives.

1

THE GOOD, THE BAD AND THE UGLY

The place where an animal or a plant lives is called its *habitat*. Animals and plants are specially suited to a particular type of habitat.

The Harvest Mouse

The Harvest Mouse is a very small animal. Its body is about 10 cm long and it weighs about 6g. It has a rusty yellow coat and large black eyes. The Harvest Mouse is active all the time, running about and skilfully climbing plant stems. It often lives in overgrown marshes, in reed beds, in damp meadows or in wet cornfields. It builds a neat round nest of woven grass leaves which hangs about 50 cm from the ground in reeds or tall grasses.

The Mole Rat

Body length — 20 cm
Tail — very small
Weight — about 200 g

The Mole Rat has a tube-shaped body covered with thick short hair. Its eyes are almost completely overgrown with fur—so that it is blind. Its eyes can only detect air currents. The Mole Rat's ears are just holes—they have no ear flaps sticking out. It has a flat head with huge sharp pointed front teeth and very hard whiskers on its cheeks. It lives in underground tunnels and uses large flat front claws to remove the soil. The Mole Rat feeds on plant roots and bulbs.

4. Make a list of FIVE things which make the Mole Rat suited to life underground.

1. Why do you think the Harvest Mouse has a rusty yellow coat?

2. Use the information in the passage and in the picture to pick out THREE things that help the Harvest Mouse to climb the stems of plants.

3. Some of the habitats of the Harvest Mouse are likely to flood. What behaviour does it show that would help it to survive a flood?

RAT FACTS

Rat catchers were very common in the past. They killed rats with arsenic and mercury poisons.

A CLIMB Rats can climb through small holes, up and along wires and inside drainpipes. They climb brick walls and up trees.

B FALL Rats can drop 20 metres without injury.

C BURROW Rats can burrow 1 metre into soil.

D GNAW Rats gnaw through a variety of materials including lead, aluminium, glass and some types of concrete!

E BREED Rats breed quickly. From a single pair, 150 rats might be bred in one year!

F SMELL Rats can smell food easily.

G SWIM Rats are excellent swimmers. They can swim at least 1000 metres and often against a current.

H Rats like something stationary next to one side of them. This is why they like to walk close to walls above ground or in sewers.

I JUMP Rats can jump 1 metre high and 1½ metres along.

The Common Rat

Wherever there are people there are rats. Rats like to live in warehouses and farms, on refuse tips and even in sewers.

Rats feed on our food and are not afraid to attack animals bigger than themselves—even humans. Rats carry diseases.

5. Why do you think that many people are afraid of rats?

6. Rats have invaded our habitat. They could live in your school or even your house. Use all the information you have about rats to design a school or a house that is completely rat proof.

You have read about three different animals which are very well suited to the habitat they live in.

7. Your task now is to design a SUPER RAT—a rat which is perfectly suited to living in a jungle habitat. Draw a picture of your rat. Explain five things that make your rat well suited to the jungle.

3

2 WHAT MAKES A WEED SUCCESSFUL?

A weed is a plant that is growing in the wrong place! Every year farmers and gardeners spend a lot of time, effort and money trying to control them because –

- weeds compete with the plants people want to grow, mainly for moisture, but also for nutrients and light;
- weeds can provide homes for pests which damage garden vegetables and other crop plants;
- if weeds are not controlled one year they will produce seeds, and this means that next year there may be even more weeds;
- weeds can spoil the appearance of a garden.

One of the best known garden weeds is the dandelion. Students in one class collected information over a year about 100 dandelion plants in the school grounds.

1. Explain what could happen to crop plants when weeds compete with them.

2. What is meant by the saying "one year seeding means seven years weeding"?

Dandelions were found growing on a wide variety of different soil types

On average, the dandelions made five flower heads each time they flowered

On average, there were 125 "seeds" in each dandelion clock

Dandelions have deep tap roots which were difficult to pull up without breaking

Each dandelion plant flowered twice that year

The students knew that many weedkillers have little or no effect on dandelions

Dandelions growing in shady places were taller than those growing in the open

New dandelion plants were able to grow from quite small pieces of tap root

The dandelion is regarded as a very successful weed.

3. What does the term "successful weed" mean? How could you measure a weed's success?

4. Give FOUR reasons for a dandelion's success.

The students took 50 "seeds" from one dandelion "clock" and sowed them in compost in a seed tray. The tray was watered thoroughly and kept in a warm airy place. Three weeks later they counted the number of seedlings that had grown (germinated). There were fewer than 50!

5. Count up the seedlings. What percentage of seeds grew into seedlings?

6. The students suggested several reasons for the "missing" seedlings:

    - Something was wrong with some of the seeds.
    - Some seeds didn't get the right conditions for germination.
    - Some of the seeds had been eaten by something.

    Are all of these possible? Which one do you think is most likely?

7. Describe how you would find out which explanation was correct. (You will need a different experiment to test each explanation.)

Weed control

The students discussed six different ways of controlling dandelions in the school grounds:

(A) Picking off the flower heads as soon as they appear.

(B) Hiring a mechanical cultivator (rotavator).

(C) Digging the whole plant out by hand.

(D) Using a "total weedkiller" (kills *all* plants and stops any plant growth for up to a year after treatment, e.g. chlorate or Pathclear).

(E) Using a contact weedkiller (kills any green plant it touches which is photosynthesising, but is quickly destroyed in soil, e.g. Paraquat or Diquat).

(F) Using a selective weedkiller (kills broad-leaved plants but not grasses, e.g. 2,4D).

8. Dandelions were a problem in three areas of the school grounds. Copy out and complete the table below to show which methods you would choose and why.

AREA OF SCHOOL GROUNDS	METHOD(S) CHOSEN	REASONS FOR CHOICE
Vegetable patch		
Lawns and playing fields		
Drive and hard tennis court		

3 SPOTTING THE DIFFERENCE

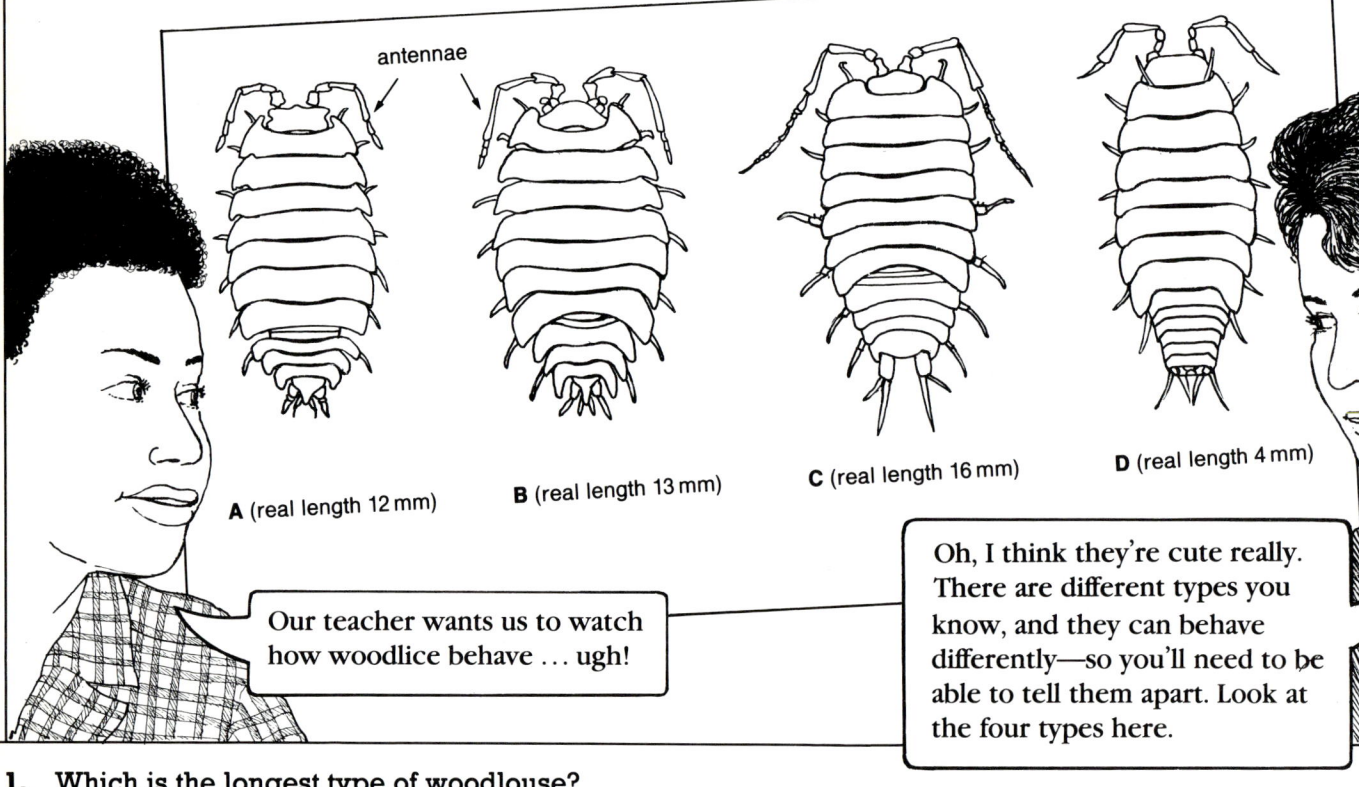

antennae

A (real length 12 mm) B (real length 13 mm) C (real length 16 mm) D (real length 4 mm)

"Our teacher wants us to watch how woodlice behave ... ugh!"

"Oh, I think they're cute really. There are different types you know, and they can behave differently—so you'll need to be able to tell them apart. Look at the four types here."

1. Which is the longest type of woodlouse?

2. Look at the antennae of A and B. How are they different? Find two other differences between A and B.

3. Find four differences between woodlice C and D.

Racing Woodlice

Now that we know how to tell them apart we can race them! We put one woodlouse in a petri dish for one minute and counted every time it crossed a heavy line—the more lines it crossed the faster it was going. We did this 3 times in the light and 3 times in semi-darkness. Look at our results.

Petri dish — Heavy lines — Graph paper

NUMBER OF HEAVY LINES CROSSED		
	SEMI – DARKNESS	LIGHT
TEST 1	‖‖‖‖ ‖‖‖‖ ‖‖‖ — 13	‖‖‖‖ ‖‖‖‖ ‖‖‖‖ ‖‖‖‖ ‖‖‖‖
TEST 2	‖‖‖‖ ‖‖‖‖ ‖‖ — 12	‖‖‖‖ ‖‖‖‖ ‖‖‖‖ ‖‖‖‖ ‖‖‖‖ ‖‖‖‖
TEST 3	‖‖‖‖ ‖‖‖‖ ‖‖‖‖ ‖‖‖‖ — 20	‖‖‖‖ ‖‖‖‖ ‖‖‖‖ ‖‖‖‖ ‖‖‖
AVERAGE	15	?

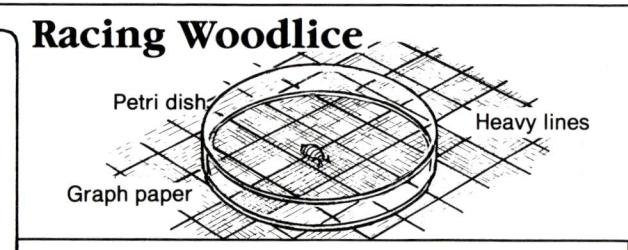

4. Work out the test totals for the number of lines crossed when tested with light.

5. What was the average for the three tests in the light?

6. Did the woodlice move about more in the dark than in the light? How do our results show this?

7. Would you expect to get exactly the same results every time you did this experiment? Explain your answer.

What makes a good experiment?

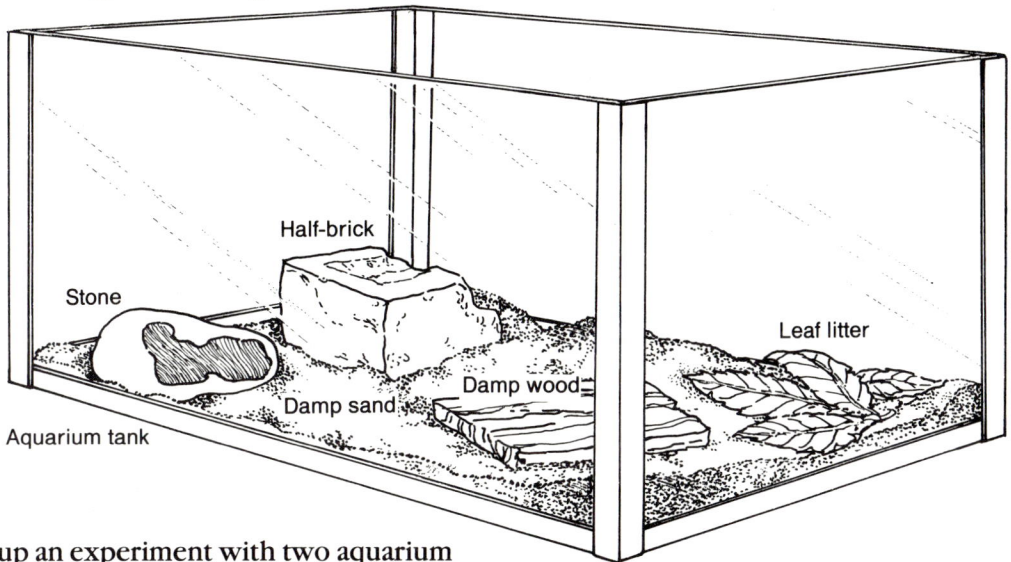

The teacher set up an experiment with two aquarium tanks. Ten woodlice were put in each tank. One tank was placed in the light, the other in the dark. Both tanks were left for 10 minutes.

The experiment was supposed to find out what sort of habitat woodlice prefer. The results are shown in the table on the right.

WHERE THE WOODLICE WERE AFTER 10 MINUTES		
PLACE	IN LIGHT	IN DARK
Under stones and bricks	3	2
In leaf litter	2	0
In the open	0	4
Under the wood	5	4

8. Suggest why more woodlice were in the open in the tank left in the dark.

I don't think this is a good experiment.

I agree!—but can you tell me why it's not good?

The pupils asked lots of questions about the experiment:

- Would woodlice "settle down" in just 10 minutes?
- What if some were hungry?
- Had they been kept in the SAME conditions before the experiment?
- Were they all the same species? Could this make a difference?
- Apart from the light being different, were the two tanks EXACTLY the same? What about dampness and temperature?

9. Make a list of the things that could have been wrong with the experiment. For each thing, say why it is important.

10. Write down clearly the things YOU would check or change to improve this experiment.

11. From what you have learned about woodlice in the light and in the dark, suggest how their behaviour could help them to survive in the wild.

4 ON THE BEACH

Garton School, Avon.

Dear Scientists,

We have just returned from our school expedition to a remote island off the coast of Scotland called Handa. Most of the field work we did was on the beach. We saw many animals and plants that we had never seen before.

Our teachers didn't know the names of all of them. They have set us the task of sorting them into groups. They say that we need to do this because knowing what a group a living thing belongs to can tell us a lot about the way it lives.

Our teachers wouldn't let us bring back any of the living things we found. We took photographs instead.

Can you help us with our work by telling us what groups these animals and plants belong to?

Thanks, the team
Deb, Phil, Raj, Steve and Terry.

1. Why do you think the teachers wouldn't let the team bring any of the living things back from the expedition?

2. Why is it useful for scientists to know what animals and plants there are on a bathing beach?

The place where animals and plants live is called a **habitat**. All the living things shown here are well suited to living on a beach or rocky shore habitat.

3. The scientist said that the team had already mentioned the two largest groups of living things in their letter. Which two groups did they mention?

4. Copy out this table. Use the information given by the scientist and in the pictures to help you to fill it in.

Name of Group	Key feature of things in this group	Example	Main clue you used to decide it belongs to this group
Coelenterates	Very soft bodies and tentacles	10	Soft body

Marine Research Laboratories,
Farley,
Devon

Dear Team,

Your teachers are quite right. Good scientists do sort living things into groups. Now you can try doing it for yourselves.

In fact, you have already mentioned the two largest groups of living things in your letter.

Here are details of some groups. You should be able to sort all your collection into these groups.

FLOWERING PLANTS: plants that produce flowers and seeds. They can be big or small.

MOSSES: plants that have simple leaves but no roots.

FERNS: plants that have proper roots and stems. Often have a broad leaf-like shape. They don't have flowers.

ALGAE: Simple plants which do not have leaves, stems or roots. They live in water.

COELENTERATES: Animals with no backbone. They have simple, very soft bodies with tentacles. Their tentacles often sting.

MOLLUSCS: Animals with no backbone, and no legs. They have smooth bodies with no segments. In many cases the body is enclosed in a shell.

ECHINODERMS: Animals with no backbone. Their body is based on five parts and they often have spines.

ARTHROPODS: Animals with no backbone. They have a body which has a hard skin and is divided into sections. Their legs have joints.

FISHES: Animals with a backbone. They live in water and have fins.

MAMMALS: Animals with backbones. They have have fur or hair. They have lungs for breathing air.

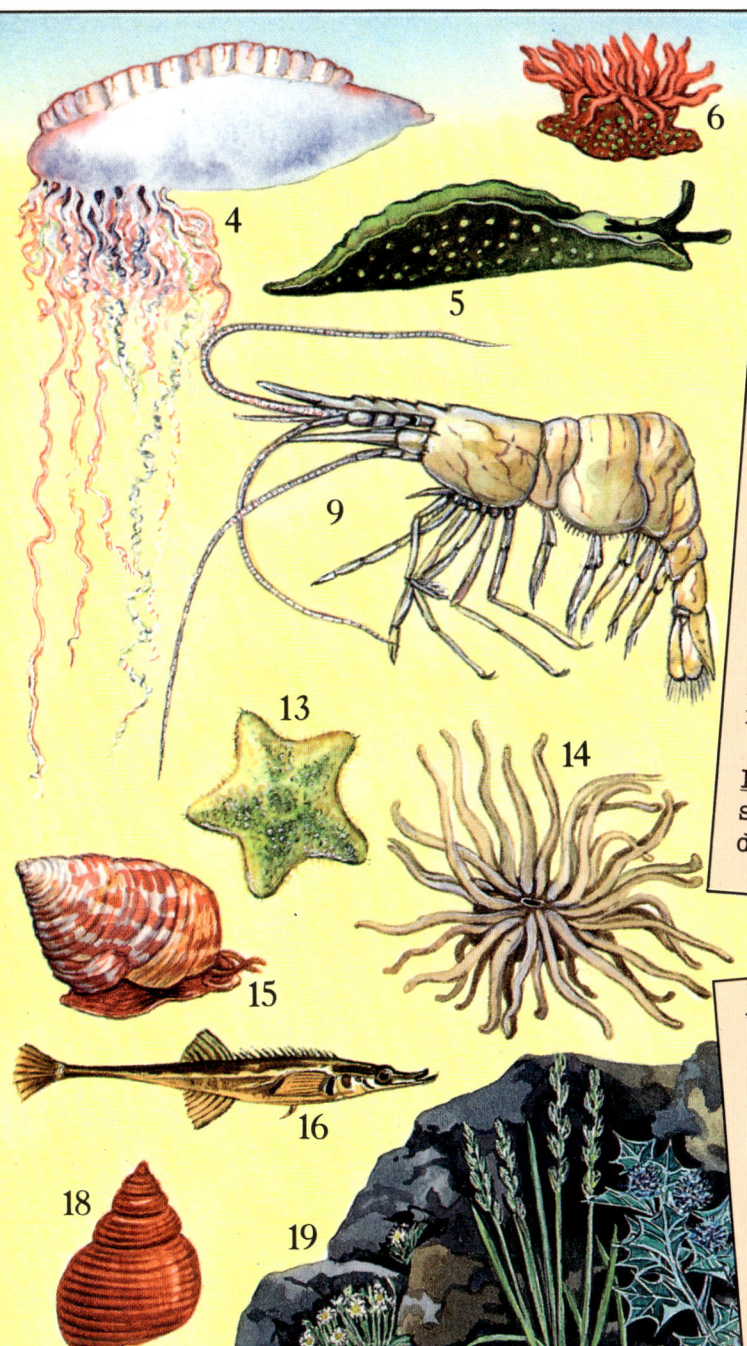

Now try to do the team's homework questions.

5. Why:
   (a) do jelly fish have stinging tentacles?

   (b) do mosses have to live in damp places?

   (c) do crabs have powerful front claws?

   (d) are many fish that live in shallow waters flat and sandy coloured?

   (e) do many molluscs have shells?

   (f) must algae live in water?

5
SUPER HUMAN!

The human body is very complex. It is organised into different parts, each part doing a special job.

BRAIN The brain controls how the body works.

EYES, EARS AND NOSE These help us to find out about the world around us.

NERVES carry messages between the brain and the rest of the body.

LUNGS Nearly all living things need oxygen. We get our oxygen through our lungs.

The HEART is a pump. It pumps blood all around the body. One of the jobs done by blood is carrying oxygen to all parts of the body.

The STOMACH works with many other organs that are not shown here. It helps break down food.

KIDNEYS remove waste materials from blood.

The BLADDER stores the liquid waste produced by the kidneys. The bladder is emptied when we go to the toilet.

MUSCLES cause movement. They can shorten, and when they do they pull on bones, causing them to move.

BONES are our support system. They hold us up, allow us to move and protect some delicate parts of the body.

BLOOD VESSELS carry blood around the body. The blood contains all the things that the parts of the body need to work.

SKIN helps to control our body temperature and is sensitive to touch and pain.

1. One of the jobs of bones is to protect delicate parts of the body. What parts of the body do the ribs protect?

2. Sometimes two or even three parts of the body work together to do one job. See if you can find FIVE examples of this. Here is one to get you started. "The lungs and the heart work together to get oxygen into and then around the body".

3. Why are there tubes connecting the kidneys to the bladder?

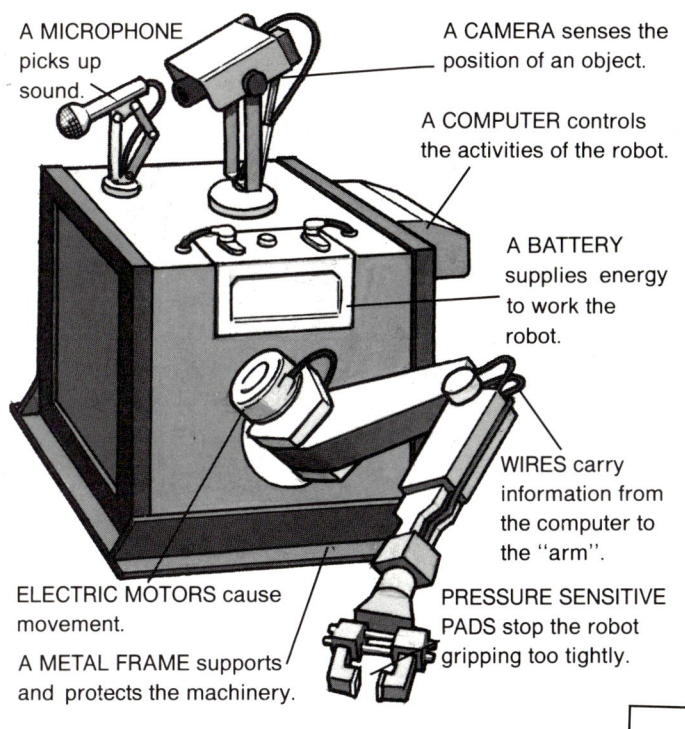

A MICROPHONE picks up sound.

A CAMERA senses the position of an object.

A COMPUTER controls the activities of the robot.

A BATTERY supplies energy to work the robot.

WIRES carry information from the computer to the "arm".

ELECTRIC MOTORS cause movement.

A METAL FRAME supports and protects the machinery.

PRESSURE SENSITIVE PADS stop the robot gripping too tightly.

The human body is so good at doing some jobs that it has been copied by scientists who build ROBOTS.

Many of the parts of the robot can be matched with the parts of the human body.

4. Copy out and complete this table.

Job	Parts of human body	Parts of robot
Movement control	Muscles	Electric motor
Carry messages		
Support		
Sensing		

5. The human body is more complex than the robot. Write down two examples of human parts not matched by parts in the robot. What jobs are done by these parts?

6. Robots are very useful. But can they replace human beings completely? Look at the list of jobs and then say whether you think each job should be done by human beings or by robots. For each answer, give a reason.

(a) Writing a poem.
(b) Testing motor cars in crashes.
(c) Bomb disposal.
(d) Playing pop music.
(e) Being a librarian.
(f) Playing sport for people to watch, e.g. tennis.
(g) Handling radioactive materials.
(h) Carrying out hospital operations.

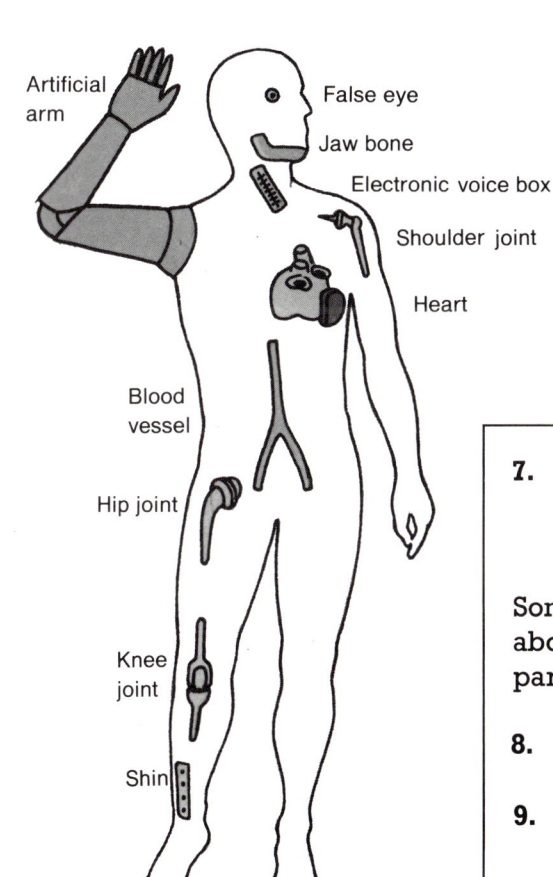

What is the difference between a human being and a robot? A human being is made of flesh and blood but a robot is made of plastic and metal. But will the difference always be so obvious?

The drawing shows some of the artificial replacements doctors can put into the human body. Scientists choose the right materials for each of the parts. An artificial arm for example is made of hard metal but is covered with a plastic which feels like our skin.

Artificial arm
False eye
Jaw bone
Electronic voice box
Shoulder joint
Heart
Blood vessel
Hip joint
Knee joint
Shin

7. What materials would you choose for the false eye, the knee joint and the artificial blood vessels? Explain why these materials are suitable.

Some scientists believe that in the future we will learn a lot more about how our bodies work and that we will be able to make all parts of the body artificially.

8. What part of the body will be most difficult to copy?

9. At what point do you think a person will stop being a human being and instead be a machine?

6 S-FACTORS

What's your favourite sport? Whatever it is, the fitter you are the better you should be at it. The four things that make up fitness are called the S-factors.

Stamina, Strength, Suppleness, and Speed (of reaction and movement).

Some students decided to measure their fitness. Here are their results:

NAME OF PUPIL	SCORES FOR Strength (kg)	Stamina	Suppleness (cm)	Speed of reaction (cm)
BOYS Varun	19.0	83	+ 11	9
Leon	25.0	61	− 7	13
Marc	25.5	75	− 1	14
Wes	31.8	90	− 7	36
GIRLS Izzy	6.5	90	+ 9	3
Karen	19.7		+ 13	8
Lisa	14.0	95	+ 14	47
Punam	8.3	55	− 8	42

To understand these results, study how each S-factor was tested.

Strength
The students held up the bathroom scales in front of them and, using just their hands, tried to "squeeze out" the highest reading possible— that's why the scores are in kg.

1. Who was the strongest?

2. Do you think this is a good test? Explain your answer.

3. Describe another test that could have been used.

Stamina
Stamina is the same as **physical endurance**. To measure this the students did "step-ups" for 4 minutes. Then their pulse rates were measured every minute for the next 3 minutes.

$$\text{Stamina score} = \frac{\text{time of exercise in seconds} \times 100}{\text{total pulse rate for 3 minutes}}$$

What the stamina scores mean
Superior   91 and over
Excellent   81–90
Good   71–80
Fair   61–70
Poor   51–60
Very poor   50 and below

4. Karen's three pulse readings were 110, 100 and 90. This means that her score was 24 000 divided by 300. Work out her **stamina score**.

5. Who had the lowest stamina score?

6. Why does someone with a low pulse rate have an advantage in this test?

Suppleness

The students stood on a bench and tried to touch their toes. Lisa's score was +14 because she could stretch 14 centimetres below the top of the bench—she was the most supple. People who couldn't reach the bench got a "minus" score. Even when he was trying his hardest, Leon's fingertips were still 7 cm above the bench, so he scored −7.

7. What would the score be for just reaching the top of the bench?

8. Lisa thought that girls are always more supple than boys, but Izzy thought this was only true *on average*. Work out the averages for the boys and for the girls. Who was right? Explain your answer.

Guess who this is

9 cm

Speed of reaction

One person lets a ruler drop—the other person catches the ruler as soon as he or she can.

9. On average the ruler fell 36 cm before Wes caught it but only 8 cm for Karen. Which of these had a faster speed of reaction? Who had the fastest reactions of all eight pupils?

10. Who had faster reactions—the boys or the girls? Explain how you reached your answer.

11. Each person had several goes before getting an average score. Explain why this would produce more accurate results.

12. Izzy's results were incredibly fast compared with the others. Do you think her reactions were really that fast? How could you improve the test?

The table shows how different sports help you improve your fitness.

1 = no real effect
2 = a little effect
3 = good effect
4 = excellent effect

Sport	Strength	Stamina	Suppleness	Speed
Badminton	2	2	3	2
Cycling (hard)	3	4	2	1
Dancing (disco)	1	3	3	1
Football	3	3	3	3
Swimming	4	4	4	2
Weight-lifting	4	1	1	1

13. Which of these sports is best for improving your general fitness? Explain how you made your choice.

14. Draw up a table to show what S-factor scores you would expect for squash, cricket and gymnastics. Explain how you decided on these scores.

15. The body is made up of several organ systems. In a healthy person these different organ systems work efficiently together. Which S-factor score would indicate a healthy

   (a) nervous system?

   (b) blood circulation system?

7
HAVING CHILDREN

Most couples decide at some stage to have children. There are many reasons for wanting children. Some are listed on the right.

1. Put these reasons for wanting children into **your** order of importance.

2. Explain why the first reason in your list is important to you.

3. Explain why you thought the last one in your list is not a good reason for having children.

(a) Having children will bring more money into the family.
(b) Everybody else seems to have children. It wouldn't look normal if we didn't.
(c) We will enjoy children.
(d) Having children means there is someone to inherit all your things.
(e) Children will be company for us when we are older.
(f) When we are very old our children can look after us.
(g) Having children is a status symbol—we can show our children off to other people.
(h) Children will bring me and my partner close together.
(i) We will find bringing up children interesting and challenging.

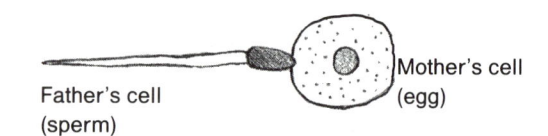

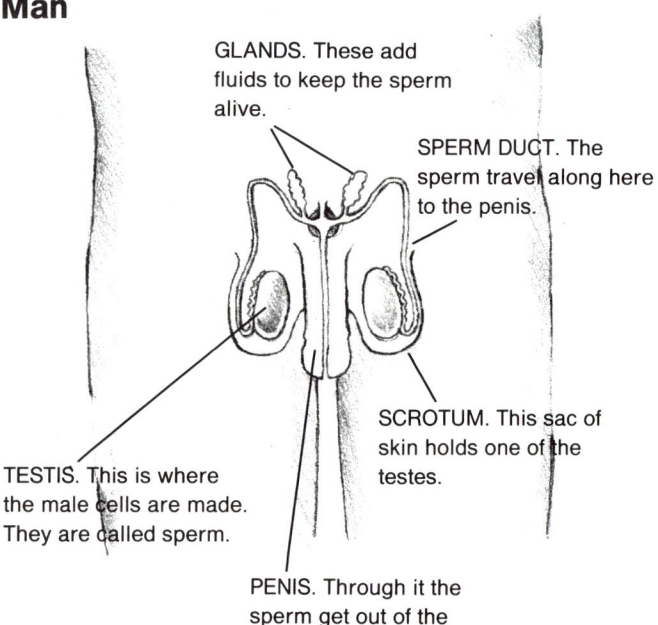

Children often look like their mother and father. This is because each parent produces a special cell containing important substances that make up the 'genes', and genes carry the information needed to form a baby. When the two cells meet they join together and a new cell is formed. This is the beginning of the new life.

Males and females have different organs that make these cells.

Father's cell (sperm)   Mother's cell (egg)

Woman

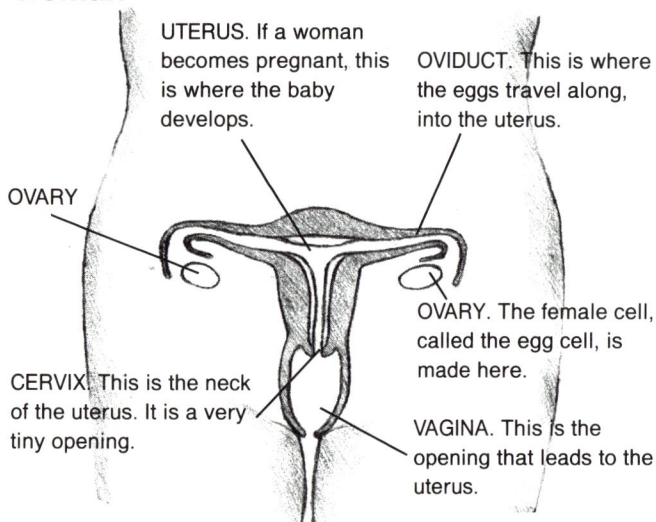

UTERUS. If a woman becomes pregnant, this is where the baby develops.

OVIDUCT. This is where the eggs travel along, into the uterus.

OVARY

OVARY. The female cell, called the egg cell, is made here.

CERVIX. This is the neck of the uterus. It is a very tiny opening.

VAGINA. This is the opening that leads to the uterus.

Man

GLANDS. These add fluids to keep the sperm alive.

SPERM DUCT. The sperm travel along here to the penis.

SCROTUM. This sac of skin holds one of the testes.

TESTIS. This is where the male cells are made. They are called sperm.

PENIS. Through it the sperm get out of the man's body.

4. Sometimes people cannot have children. Study the diagrams above and make a list of things that might go wrong in the man and the woman that could stop them having children.

(1)

(2)

(3)

(4)

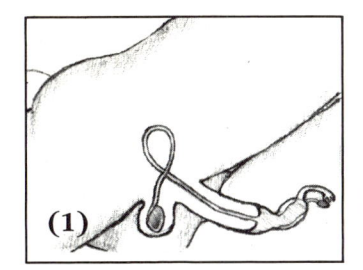

(A) The cells divide and form a ball of cells. This settles into the lining of the uterus. The ball of cells continues dividing. The cells grow and become more complicated.

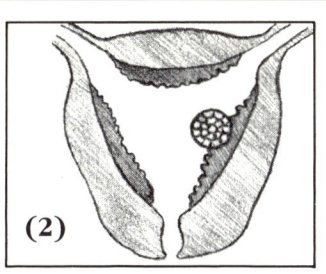

(B) Many thousands of sperm are released but only a few hundred survive the journey and reach the egg. One sperm joins the egg to form a new cell.

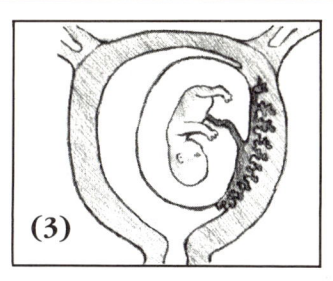

(C) The penis is put inside the female's vagina. The sperm are released. They swim through the cervix into the uterus and on towards the egg.

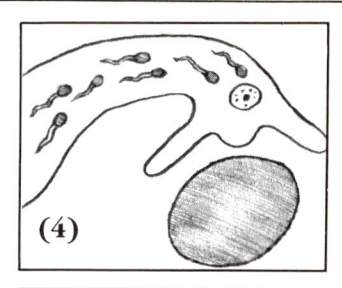

(D) By three months the ball of cells has changed into a miniature person with arms and legs. It grows inside the mother for about 9 months.

5. The pictures above show some important stages in the development of a baby. The pictures and writing do not match and they are not in the right order. Match the writing to the pictures and then put them in the right order.

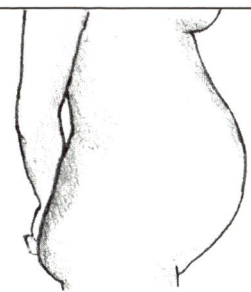

For nine months the baby is carried inside the mother. Lots of things can affect the baby during this time and the mother needs to take great care.

6. Think of FIVE things the mother should or shouldn't do when she is pregnant.

When a child is born it needs a lot of looking after. We usually look after our children until they are in their late teens.

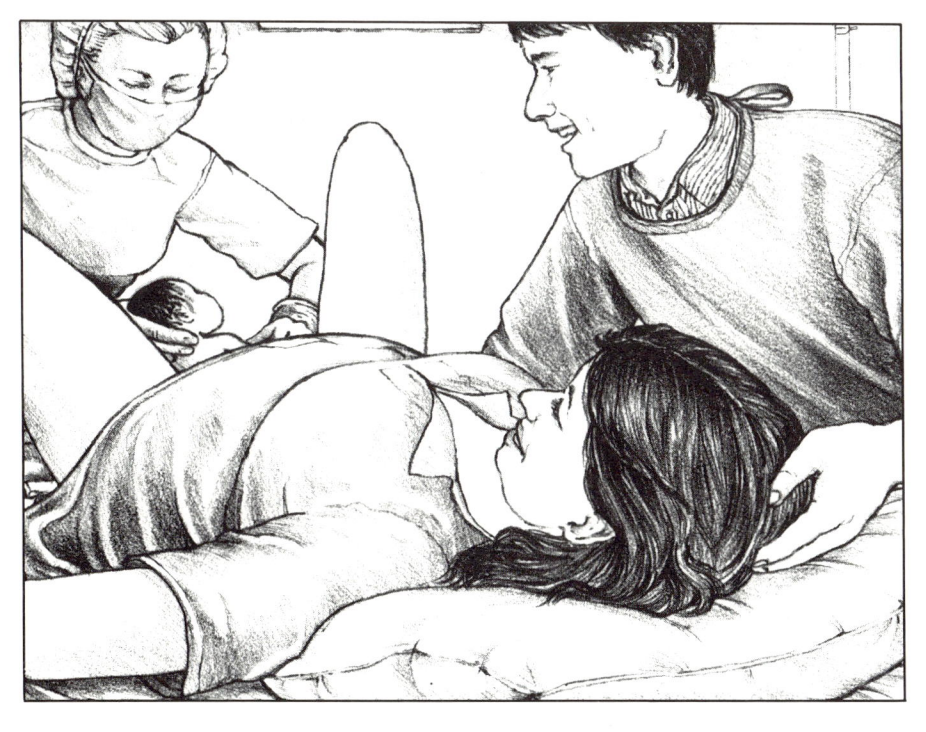

7. This couple have just had their first child, a baby boy. What preparations should they have made? Write down THREE changes they should make to their lives.

8. What difference might it make if the mother were on her own?

15

8
THE RIGHT CHOICE

My name is Sokhraj. I've chosen steak pie, mash and beans. I like a stodgy meal to fill me up.

My name is Paul. I love hamburger and chips. I think I've made a good choice for my meal.

I'm Angela, and I like meals with rice. I've chosen chicken risotto and cabbage. Have I made a good choice?

The table on the right shows what is in a normal portion of each of the foods in the meals chosen by the pupils. It also shows how much of each substance is present.

1. People take much more notice of advice like "eat less fat" than they used to. If you agree with all the headlines, then some meals are a "good" choice and some are a "bad" choice.

   Copy and complete these sentences:

   "A good meal is one which contains a lot of _____ but little _____."

   "A bad meal is one which contains a lot of _____ but little _____."

2. Which headline do the experts disagree about?

FOOD	Protein	Fat	Starch	Sugar	Salt	Vitamins and minerals	Fibre
Beefburger	✓✓✓	✓✓✓	✓	✓	✓✓	✓	X
Steak	✓✓✓	✓✓	X	X	X	✓✓	X
Chicken	✓✓✓	✓	X	X	X	✓✓	X
Ham	✓✓✓	✓✓	X	X	X	✓✓	X
Bread bun (white)	✓✓	✓	✓✓✓	✓	✓	✓✓	✓
Rice (white)	✓✓	✓	✓✓✓	X	✓	✓	✓
Pastry	✓✓	✓✓✓	✓✓✓	✓	✓	✓✓	✓
Chips	✓	✓✓✓	✓✓✓	X	X	✓	X
Potato salad	✓	✓✓	✓✓✓	✓	✓	✓	X
Mashed potato	✓	X	✓✓✓	X	✓	✓	X
Baked beans	✓✓	✓	✓	✓✓	✓✓	✓✓	✓✓✓
Cabbage	✓	X	✓	X	✓	✓✓✓	✓✓✓
Lettuce	✓	X	✓	X	X	✓✓✓	✓✓✓
Apple	✓	X	X	✓	X	✓	✓✓

Key: X = none   ✓ = very little   ✓✓ = a fair amount   ✓✓✓ = a lot

Hi, I'm Julie. I like salads. This is a ham salad. I think I've made a good choice of meal.

PEOPLE IN BRITAIN EAT TOO MUCH SUGAR
Some doctors have started to advise patients suffering from heart disease that they could be eating too much sugar.

BRITISH DIETS CONTAIN TOO LITTLE FIBRE
Doctors argue that some problems with the gut can be avoided if people eat more fibre. Diseases such as bowel cancer, constipation and

TOO MUCH SALT EATEN IN BRITAIN
A report published today claims that the average person eats too much salt. Some experts think that problems with the heart and

Other experts say that the evidence does not support claims that high salt intake

PEOPLE EAT TOO MUCH FAT
A strong link between high fat diets and heart attacks is suggested by evidence in a report out today.

CHILDREN'S DIETS TOO LOW IN VITAMINS
Doctors are worried that children in many areas are not getting enough vitamins and minerals in their diets. They blame the choices of meals made

Vitamins and minerals are needed to keep the body healthy. Without enough of them in the diet, diseases can result

3. Copy out the table below.

MEAL	WHAT IS BAD ABOUT IT	WHAT IS GOOD ABOUT IT
Steak pie, mash, baked beans	Lots of sugar. Quite a lot of salt.	Lots of vitamins and minerals. Lots of protein. Lots of fibre. Lots of starch. Not much fat.

Complete the table with the meals chosen by the pupils. Decide on the good and bad points for each meal. Add this information to the table. The first meal has been done for you.

4. Which meals do you think are a good choice?

5. In your school there will be people who do not make the right choice. Plan a campaign to persuade them to make a good choice of meal in future. Here are some questions you could think about to get you started.

- What would you put on a poster advertising the campaign?
- What kinds of extra information could you find out to back you up?
- Will you want to talk to an expert? If so, who?
- Do you want an expert to talk to your school?
- Would you use a questionnaire to find out what people eat?

9
MOUTH MATTERS

PLAQUE!
If you don't clean your teeth you will notice that you get a "furry feeling" on your teeth. This is plaque. It is a soft coating made up of millions of bacteria. It builds up on teeth, especially near the gums.

TOOTH DECAY
The sugar in the foods you eat is used by the bacteria in plaque to form an acid. The acid attacks the enamel and causes holes in it.

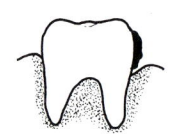

GUM DISEASE
If plaque is not removed it will build up around the gums. This causes swelling and bleeding of the gums. If this is allowed to continue teeth become weak and can be lost.

FOUR RULES OF ORAL HYGIENE
1. Brush your teeth using toothpaste. This removes the plaque. If there is fluoride in the toothpaste it strengthens the enamel.

2. Eat foods that are low in sugar.

3. Visit your dentist regularly. Your dentist will clean and repair your teeth.

4. Use dental floss or wooden sticks to clean in between your teeth.

COMPETITION
Are your teeth healthy?

What is plaque?

Why is a lot of sugar in your food bad for your teeth?

- The four rules of hygiene are not in any order. Decide what order you think they should go in and say why.

- Complete this slogan. "Brushing teeth matters because ...".

Sharon and Paul are visiting the dentist. The waiting room walls are covered with posters.

1. The last poster advertises a competition. Use all the information from the other three posters to answer the questions in the competition.

Paul has listened to advice about how to look after his teeth. He brushes his teeth twice a day. Sharon has been lazy. Now as she sits in the waiting room she is feeling nervous.

When Sharon enters the surgery she relaxes a little. There is pop music playing, and the walls have interesting pictures to look at.

2. Why do you think dentists often play music and have interesting pictures on the walls of their surgeries?

The dentist began by examining Sharon's top jaw.

Dentists keep records of the state of your teeth and of the treatments you need. These records are kept in the form of a code on a chart. Here is an example of a dentist's chart.

The top line of the chart is filled in with code for the state of the teeth when they are examined. Here is an example of the code.

Code for the state of the teeth	
Ordinary tooth present code	●
Existing filling	●
A cavity in the tooth	○
Tooth is missing	/

Dentists need to record what fillings you need. They read out to an assistant the number of the tooth, the existing details of that tooth and where the filling is needed. The assistant records this in the code used below.

NAME							DATE
UPPER JAW RIGHT SIDE							
Tooth number	1	2	3	4	5	6	7
Existing details	●	●	○	○	○	●	○
Type of filling needed	—	—	0	0	P	—	OT

UPPER JAW LEFT SIDE							
Tooth number	1	2	3	4	5	6	7
Existing details							
Type of filling needed							

Surface of tooth	Code	Name	Where the filling is needed
	O	Occlusal	On the top of the tooth
	B	Buccal	On the cheek side of the tooth
	P	Palatal	On the inside of the tooth
	OT	Other type	To cover two surfaces

FACT
Tooth disease is the world's commonest disease.

FACT
Most people lose some of their teeth because of gum disease.

FACT
Few people manage to reach old age without losing some or all of their teeth.

FACT
With proper care your teeth SHOULD be yours for life.

Do you remember me telling you about having a brace on my teeth? Well I went to the dental hospital today to have it removed! It's funny, I had almost forgotten my old nickname. That brace has been on my teeth for two years. It was a nuisance at the time. It didn't look very nice and bits of food kept getting stuck in it but it seems worth it now. I can bite my food without digging into the top of my mouth. Best of all my P.E. teacher says I can play hockey for the team now my teeth don't stick out. Even Dad is pleased. He says it was worth the money because I don't grind my teeth any more. Mum's pleased too because she thinks I will be able to keep them cleaner.

Attachment for the brace

Paul's teeth with the brace on

Paul's teeth after the brace was taken off

If you study the picture of Sharon's teeth you will see that she needs some fillings. The codes for the right side of Sharon's top jaw have already been done.

3. Copy the chart for the left side. Use the codes to fill it in.

4. Do you think Sharon's teeth are in good condition? Suggest three pieces of advice you would give to Sharon.

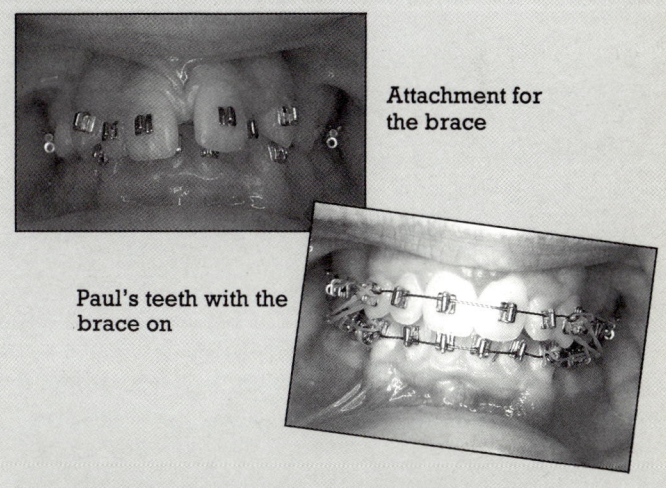

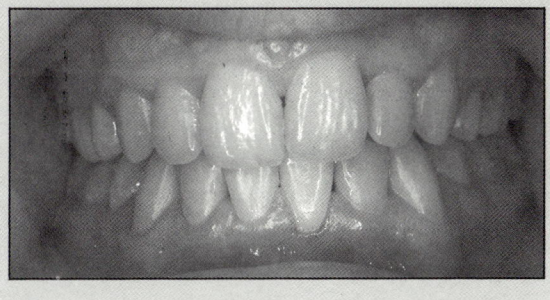

5. Paul has had a brace on his teeth. Look at the pictures before and after and write down the differences you can see in Paul's teeth.

6. Read Paul's letter to a friend. Draw up a table to show the advantages and disadvantages of having the brace on the teeth.

10
CONFINED TO THE CELL

A Bacterium

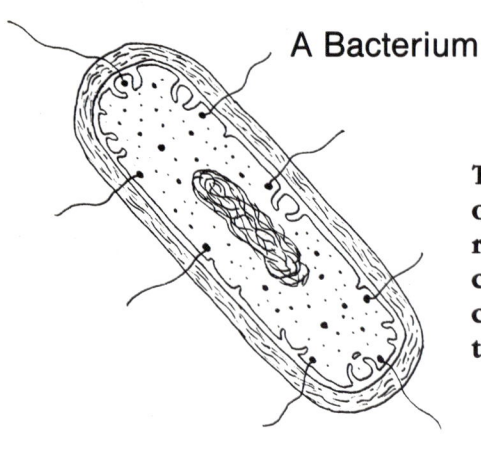

A Human

The organism on the left is just one cell. The organism on the right is made up of billions of cells. Both organisms have to carry out the same processes to stay alive.

Respiration → Getting energy out of food

Reproduction → Breeding to make new individuals

Two of the processes needed to keep humans alive

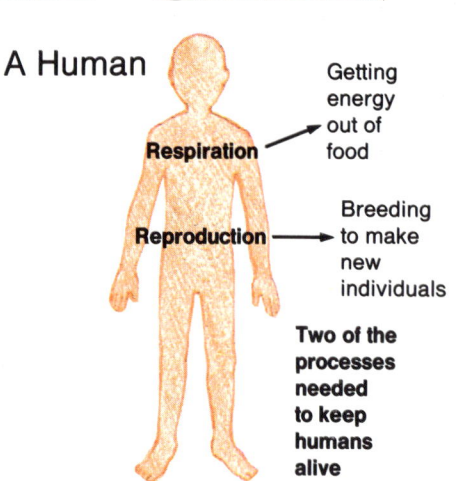

1. Write a list of all of the processes you can think of which bacteria will need to carry out in just one cell.

Some bacteria can be harmful to people. For example this one, called *Salmonella*, can cause food poisoning if it is in or on food. Its victims have diarrhoea, severe pain in their intestines, and vomit a lot.

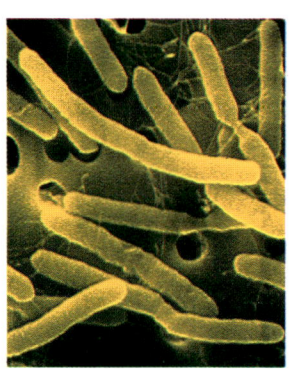

Salmonella cells on a piece of meat

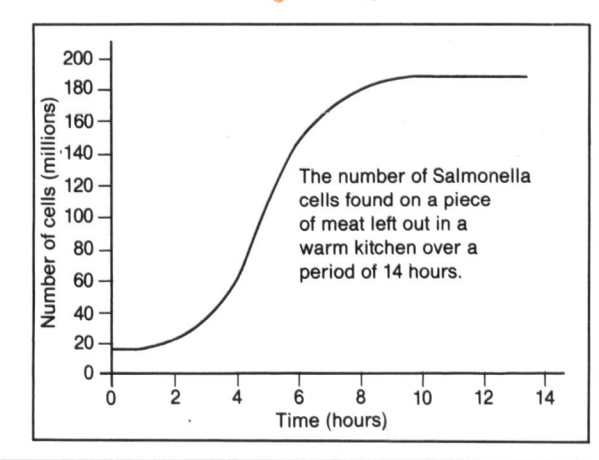

The number of Salmonella cells found on a piece of meat left out in a warm kitchen over a period of 14 hours.

2. Look at the graph (above right). During which period of time did the number of *Salmonella* cells increase most quickly?

3. If the smallest number of cells which can make somebody ill is 80 million, what is the longest time that this piece of infected meat can be left for before it is dangerous to eat?

4. Suggest THREE precautions a cook could take to prevent people getting food poisoning from *Salmonella*.

A Carrying messages...

B Attacking invaders...

C Providing movement...

D Transporting supplies...

5. The human body is made of different kinds of cells. Match each of the cell types below with the picture of the job it does.

Red blood cells in the bloodstream carry oxygen from the lungs to all parts of the body.

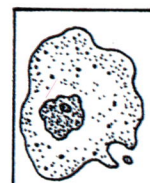

White blood cells engulf and destroy harmful microbes and remove waste particles.

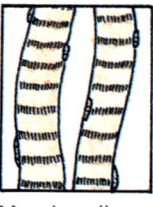

Muscle cells contract to move the bones.

Nerve cells receive and pass on messages to and from all parts of the body.

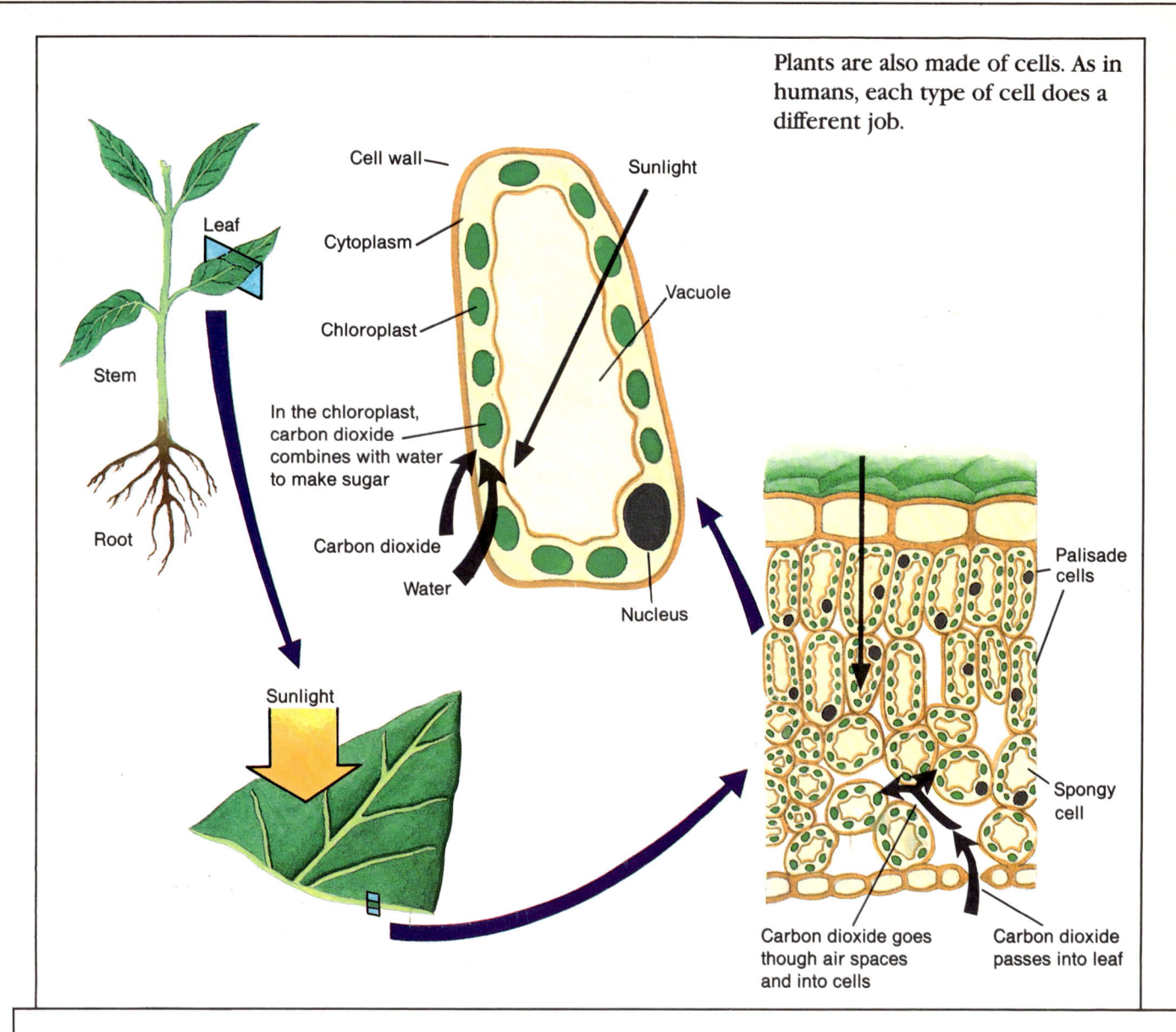

Plants are also made of cells. As in humans, each type of cell does a different job.

Labels on plant diagram: Leaf, Stem, Root

Labels on cell diagram: Cell wall, Cytoplasm, Chloroplast, Sunlight, Vacuole, Nucleus, In the chloroplast, carbon dioxide combines with water to make sugar, Carbon dioxide, Water

Labels on leaf cross-section: Sunlight, Palisade cells, Spongy cell, Carbon dioxide goes though air spaces and into cells, Carbon dioxide passes into leaf

6. Copy out this table.

Type of cell	Number of:		Average number of chloroplasts
	Cells	Chloroplasts	
Palisade			
Spongy			

7. Count the number of each type of cell in the cross-section of the leaf and write this information in the appropriate boxes in the table.

8. Count up the number of chloroplasts in all the palisade cells, and write this number in the table. Do the same for the spongy cells.

9. For each type of cell, divide the number of chloroplasts by the number of cells. Write the numbers you have calculated in the last column of the table.

10. What job is done by the chloroplasts in leaf cells?

11. Which cell type has more chloroplasts, the palisade or spongy cells?

12. Can you think of any reason why these cells have more chloroplasts in them?

13. Which surface of the leaf are these cells nearest?

14. What can these cells absorb most easily by being near this surface?

11

CORONARY HEART DISEASE

This is the heart of a person who is suffering from coronary heart disease.

One of the blood vessels which supplies oxygen and food to the heart muscle is becoming blocked. If the blood vessel becomes completely blocked, the heart muscle it supplies with blood will be starved of oxygen and the heart may stop beating. This causes a heart attack.

Surgeons can sometimes treat coronary heart disease by using a piece of blood vessel from the patient's leg. The vein is used to bypass the blockage in the coronary artery.

1. What does the blood supply to the heart muscle to provide it with a source of energy?

2. Explain the cause of a heart attack in your own words.

3. What do you think happens during a bypass operation?

Many people die of coronary heart disease. This makes it important to find out why coronary arteries become blocked. One way of looking for the causes of coronary heart disease is to find which people are most at risk of getting the disease.

This table shows the percentage of the deaths during 1980 which were caused by coronary heart disease. The information is for men and women of different ages.

AGE GROUP	25–34	35–44	45–54	55–64	65–74
Men	5	30	40	40	35
Women	3	10	15	20	30

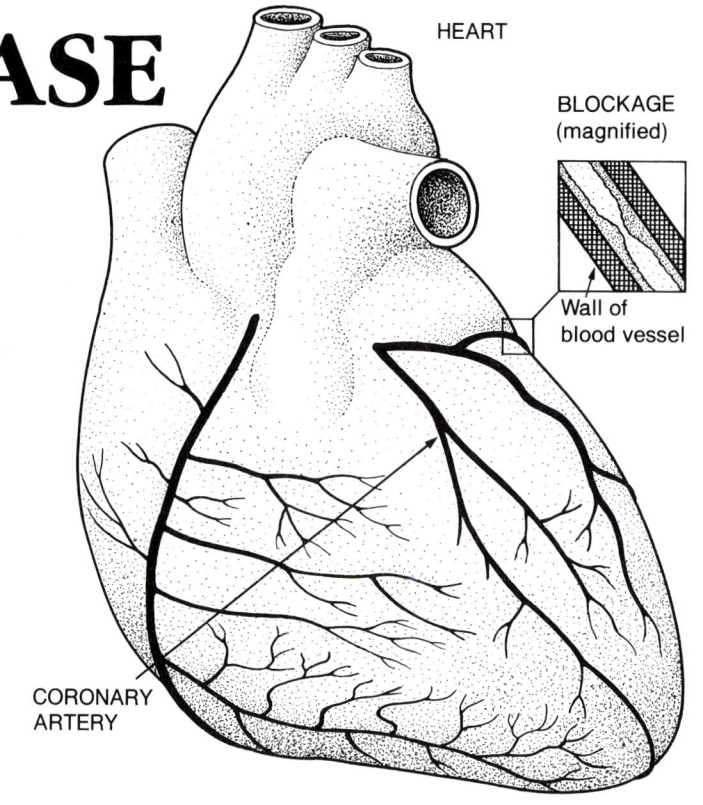

4. Draw a bar chart to show these figures more clearly. The axes you should use are shown and the first entry has been done as an example.

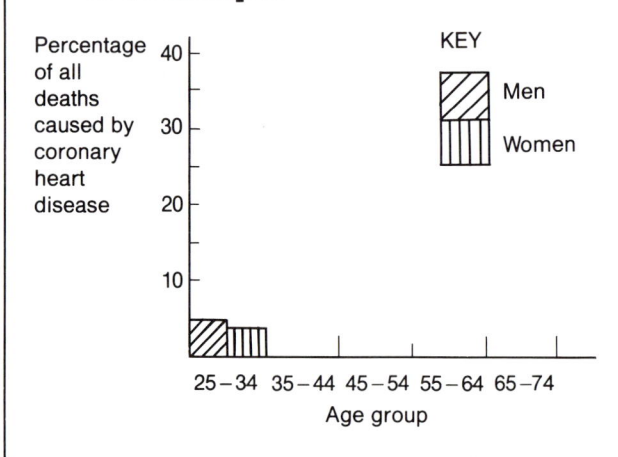

5. Are deaths from coronary heart disease more common amongst women or men?

6. In which age groups is coronary heart disease the most common cause of death for

   (a) women?

   (b) men?

Doctors believe that smoking is linked to heart disease. Study the bar chart carefully. It shows the connection between smoking and deaths from coronary heart disease. The figures are for a sample of 100 000 men aged between 40 and 45.

7. How many men in the sample who did not smoke died of coronary heart disease?

8. How many men in the sample who were heavy smokers (25 or more cigarettes a day) died of coronary heart disease?

9. Complete this sentence—"The greater the number of cigarettes a person smokes the ...."

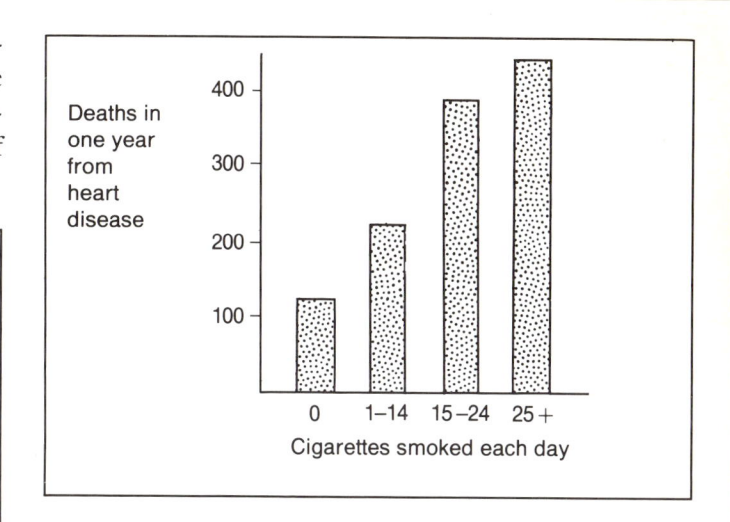

This kind of information has helped doctors to draw up a chart. The scores for each column are added together to give a total. This is used to estimate a person's risk of suffering from coronary heart disease.

The chart also shows the ways in which a person can reduce his or her risk of coronary heart disease, for example, by losing weight.

AGE	SEX	WEIGHT	BLOOD PRESSURE	% ANIMAL FAT IN DIET	EXERCISE	TOBACCO SMOKING	FAMILY HISTORY OF HEART DISEASE
10–20 (1)	Female under 40 (1)	More than 5 lb below standard weight (0)	Upper reading 100 (1)	No animal fat (1)	Hard manual job and exercise (2)	Non-smoker (0)	None (1)
21–30 (2)	Female 40–50 (2)	Within 5 lb of standard weight (1)	Upper reading 120 (2)	10% animal fat (2)	Manual job and moderate exercise (2)	Cigar or pipe smoker (1)	1 relative over 60 (2)
31–40 (3)	Female over 50 (3)	6–20 lb overweight (2)	Upper reading 140 (3)	20% animal fat (3)	Office work and hard exercise (3)	10 cigarettes a day or less (3)	2 relatives over 60 (3)
41–50 (4)	Male (5)	21–35 lb overweight (3)	Upper reading 160 (4)	30% animal fat (4)	Office work and moderate exercise (5)	20 cigarettes a day (5)	1 relative under 60 (4)
51–60 (5)	Stocky male (6)	36–50 lb overweight (5)	Upper reading 180 (6)	40% animal fat (6)	Office work and light exercise (5)	30 cigarettes a day (7)	2 relatives under 60 (6)
61 and over (8)	Bald, stocky male (7)	51 lb or more overweight (7)	Upper reading 200 or more (7)	50% animal fat (7)	No exercise at all (8)	40 cigarettes a day or more (11)	3 relatives under 60 (7)

SCORE	RISK
Less than 7	see your maths teacher as soon as possible!
7–11	well below average risk
12–17	below average risk
18–24	average risk
25–31	moderate risk
32–40	dangerous risk
41 and over	immediate danger—see your doctor!

STEPHEN
Stocky build, aged 17, 7 lb overweight, blood pressure 140 over 90, likes dairy and fried foods (50% animal fat in diet). Takes regular hard exercise but smokes 20 cigarettes a day. Two of his close relatives had heart attacks before they were 60.

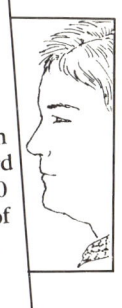

10. Which THREE factors do people have no control over?

11. Use the chart to work out the risk of Jane and Stephen developing coronary heart disease.

12. What advice would you give to each of them to improve their health?

JANE
Aged 15, correct weight for her height, blood pressure 120 over 80. Likes cream and butter but has cut animal fat in her diet down to 20%. Doesn't smoke, and her only close relative to have a heart attack was her grandad at age 75. Takes no exercise at all.

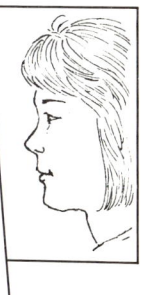

12 AEROBICS

1. Which of these two girls has just finished her aerobics class?

2. List four of the changes that occur in your body when you do strenuous exercises.

AT SCHOOL...

> Miss, why is it called aerobics?

> Because you need oxygen from the **air** to do the exercises, Sarah.

> Is that why we breathe very deeply?

> Yes, you need to take air into your lungs.

> So why does my heart rate go up?

> The oxygen passes out of your lungs into your blood. The heart pumps this **oxygenated** blood around your body.

> What does the oxygen do?

> All the cells in your body are doing special jobs. They need the energy that is stored in your food...

> The oxygen is used to release this stored energy. In the process, your food is usually turned into carbon dioxide and water.

> This process of releasing energy from food is called **respiration**.

> Now I understand. The more energetic I am, the more oxygen I need.

Sarah decided to measure her breathing rate when doing certain things. She thought that this would tell her which activity needs the most energy.

Activity	Number of breaths per minute
Walking	15
Sprinting	24
Jogging	18
Sitting at desk	14
Dancing	19
Watching T.V.	14
Aerobics	22

3. Which of the changes in your list for question 2 happen because you need to get more oxygen into your body?

4. Draw a bar chart to show the number of breaths taken each minute when Sarah did the seven different activities. On your chart you should put the least strenuous activity first.

5. Predict the number of breaths that Sarah would take each minute if she were

    (a) sleeping, (b) reading, (c) cycling.

6. Why do cells need oxygen?

7. What do you think happens to the carbon dioxide and water which is formed when you respire?

THAT EVENING...

They hardly breathe during the race. But it must take a lot of energy to run that fast.

The 100 m sprint only lasts ten seconds.

I can run up the stairs without breathing. This must take a lot of energy. How can I respire without using oxygen?

THE NEXT DAY AT SCHOOL...

Miss, when you run up the stairs or sprint you use a lot of energy, don't you?

Yes Sarah, why?

Well, when I dash up the stairs, I don't breathe! How do I get the energy without using oxygen?

That's a good question.

When you do exercise it takes time for your breathing rate and heart rate to increase.

So how do I get the energy to run up the stairs?

*Your body has a way of releasing energy from food without using oxygen. This is called **anaerobic respiration**.*

So why don't we respire like this all the time? We wouldn't have to breathe then!

In anaerobic respiration your food is turned into lactic acid. If there is too much lactic acid in your muscle cells, you get cramp.

8. Why is it difficult to get enough oxygen into our muscles during short bursts of strenuous exercise?

9. What is the disadvantage of anaerobic respiration?

An experiment was carried out to find out how good a swimmer was at respiring anaerobically. The graph shows the change in the concentration of lactic acid in the blood during and after a nine-minute race.

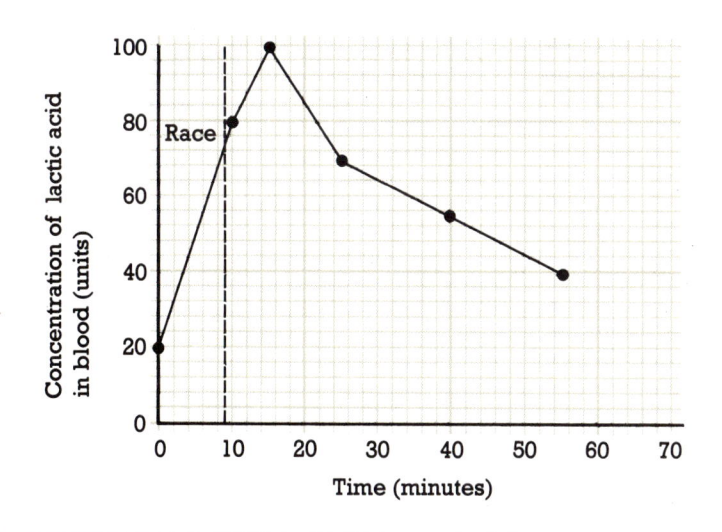

10. Why is it an advantage for a swimmer to be able to respire anaerobically?

11. What was the concentration of lactic acid in the swimmer's blood at the start of the race?

12. Describe the change in concentration of lactic acid in the blood during and after the race.

13. Predict the time needed for the concentration of lactic acid in the swimmer's blood to return to normal.

14. Suggest THREE exercises that would help an athlete to become better at respiring anaerobically.

13 GROW YOUR OWN

Two years ago, Mr and Mrs Wilson and their two children decided to turn all of their garden into a vegetable plot. They wanted to grow as much of their own food as they could.

To begin with, the Wilsons grew their crops outdoors. They found that most of them were easy to grow in the spring and summer but some were difficult to grow in the winter.

The first year was full of problems for the Wilsons—it was very hard work. However, the family were pleased with what they had achieved and they were looking forward to the next year.

1. Think of THREE reasons why the Wilsons may have wanted to grow their own food.

2. Give THREE examples of the sort of vegetables the Wilsons might have grown.

3. Why do you think the Wilsons found it more difficult to grow crops in the winter?

4. Suggest THREE problems the Wilsons might have faced in their first year when trying to grow their crops.

The Wilsons needed to increase the amount of crops they were growing and to grow the crops more quickly. One day Susan came home from school—triumphant! Susan thought that she had the answer. She showed them her science book.

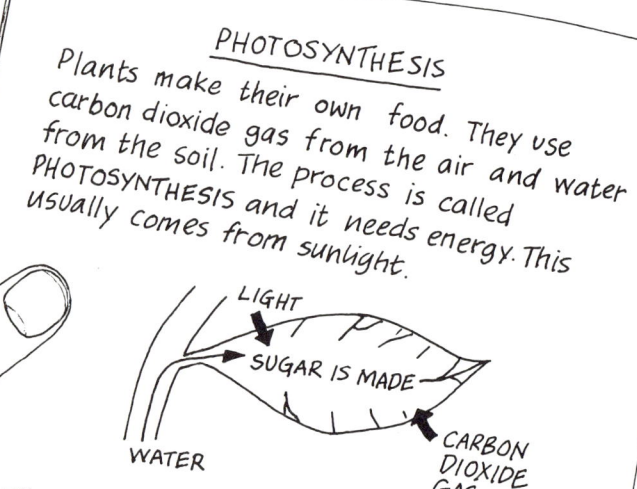

PHOTOSYNTHESIS

Plants make their own food. They use carbon dioxide gas from the air and water from the soil. The process is called PHOTOSYNTHESIS and it needs energy. This usually comes from sunlight.

LIGHT → SUGAR IS MADE
WATER
CARBON DIOXIDE GAS

The green substance in leaves called chlorophyll helps plants to trap sunlight. The food that plants make is sugar. This is used by plants as they grow. It can also be turned to starch and stored. Oxygen gas is also produced by plants during photosynthesis.

The amount of light affects photosynthesis
Amount of sugar produced vs Hours of light in 24 hours

The amount of carbon dioxide affects photosynthesis
Amount of sugar produced vs Carbon dioxide concentration

The temperature affects photosynthesis
Amount of sugar produced vs Temperature

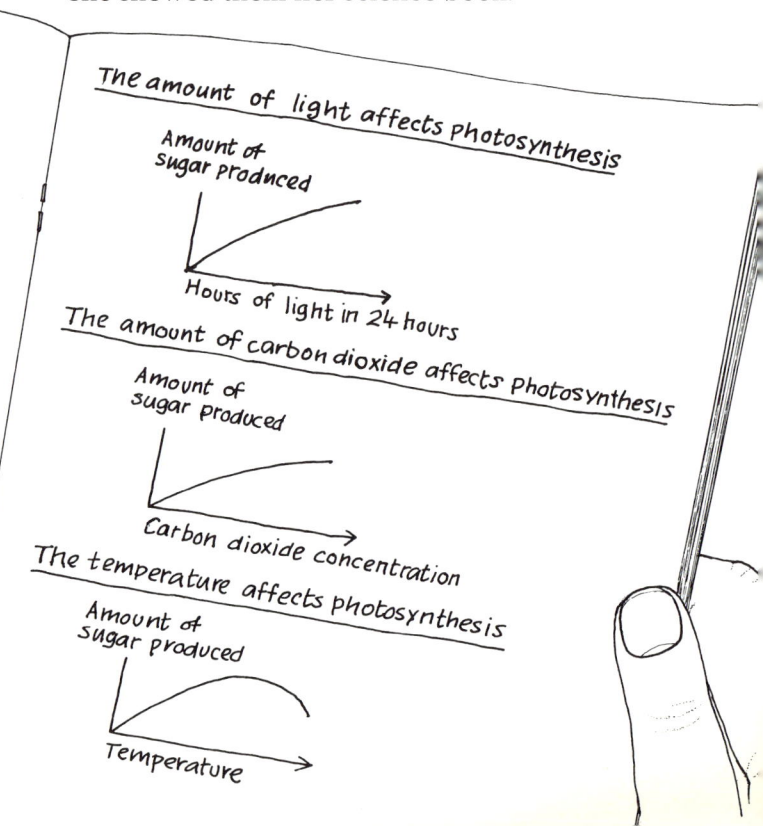

5. Make a list of the FOUR things that are used by a plant for photosynthesis.

6. Use the information in Susan's graphs to describe how the following affect the amount of sugar produced by a plant during photosynthesis:

   (a) The number of hours of sunlight in 24 hours.

   (b) The concentration of carbon dioxide in the air.

   (c) The temperature.

7. Why is this information important to the Wilsons?

The Wilsons decided that they needed to build a greenhouse, but not just an ordinary garden greenhouse! They decided that they were going to make full use of all the information in Susan's book. *Firstly*, they had to decide where to put the greenhouse. Mrs Wilson drew a plan of their garden and Mr Wilson plotted onto it the position of the path of the sun across the sky.

8. The sun rises above the middle oak tree and sets behind the sheds. Which of the sites A, B or C do you think is most suitable? Explain your answer.

The next problem was which type of greenhouse to buy. The Wilsons had two choices. The tunnel type, with metal frames and plastic sheet cover, or the traditional glasshouse with a wooden frame.

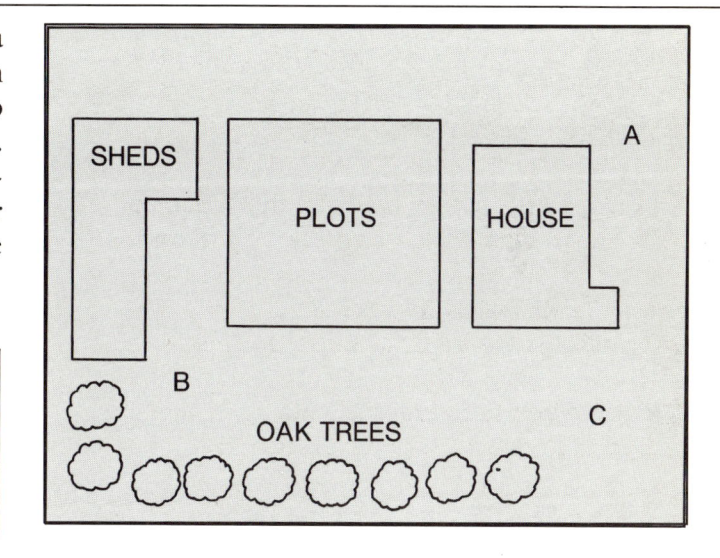

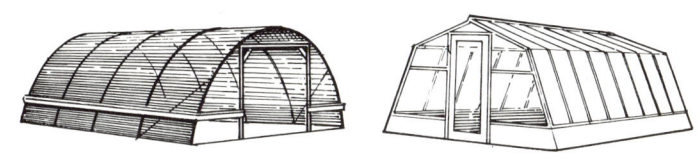

9. Write down ONE advantage and ONE disadvantage of each type of greenhouse.

10. Which one would you choose? Explain why.

11. The Wilsons want to make the best use of all of Susan's information about photosynthesis. To do this they need to make changes to the greenhouse they chose.

    Your task now is to draw up plans for their super greenhouse!

    You need:

    to increase the length of time the plants will be in light

    to keep the plants at the right temperature

    to think of a way of giving the plants more carbon dioxide

    (Clue—burning fuels like coal and gas produces carbon dioxide.)

    Remember the Wilsons want to save money. Make your greenhouse as cheap to run as possible. You also need to make it safe.

    Draw up your plans and label any equipment. Explain what the equipment is for, and why it will help to grow plants more quickly.

14

UNHAPPY HOUSEPLANTS

FLOWER BUDS FALL

Commonest causes: dry air, too little water, too little light, moving the pot, insect damage.

PLANT GROWING SLOWLY OR NOT AT ALL

Normal in Winter. In Summer, it may be caused by too much water or too little light. Pot may be too small.

1. Copy out the table below, leaving enough space to answer questions 2 and 3.

PLANT	Problem	Cause	Cure
Geranium			
Cheese Plant			
Rubber Plant			
Ivy Plant			

SMALL PALE LEAVES

Plant has been kept too warm in Winter or early Spring. If it happens in Summer it is caused by too little light or not enough nutrients in the soil.

2. Use the information in the leaves around the page to decide which problems each plant has. Fill in the "Problem" and "Cause" columns of the table you have drawn.

LEAVES TURNING YELLOW AND FALLING OFF

Usually caused by too much water or cold draughts.

Spineless Yucca — Yucca Elephantipes

Take good care of me with **FISONS** Houseplant Care Range

- **IDEAL TEMPERATURE** 7°C-12°C (41°F-55°F)
- **LIVING POSITION** Requires plenty of light, likes to be placed out of doors in Summer. Makes a good plant for a sunny patio. Does not like to be too hot and dry in Winter.
- **MOISTURE/FEEDING** Water freely in Summer, less frequently in Winter. Use *FISONS* Long Lasting Feed every 4 months or *FISONS* Deep Feed every 2 weeks during the growing season.
- **AFTERCARE** Repot once a year in *FISONS* Potting Mixture when young. After 3-4 years just remove the top compost and replace with fresh. Do not use leafshine.

Swiss Cheese Plant — Monstera Deliciosa

Take good care of me with **FISONS** Houseplant Care Range

- **IDEAL TEMPERATURE** 10°C-21°C (50°F-70°F)
- **LIVING POSITION** Indirect light best—avoid direct sunlight, will grow slowly in shady areas.
- **MOISTURE/FEEDING** Allow to dry out between watering—water more in Summer than Winter. Use *FISONS* Long-Lasting Feed every 4 months or *FISONS* Deep Feed weekly during the growing season.
- **AFTERCARE** Repot every Spring in *FISONS* Potting Mixture. Use moss poles for added effect when plant gets too tall. Spray leaves weekly with tepid water to create a tropical atmosphere—always avoid draughts. Use *FISONS* Leafshine Wipes regularly.

ROTTING LEAVES AND STEMS

Can be caused by disease or by too much water.

BROWN TIPS, EDGES OR SPOTS ON LEAVES

Caused by hot, dry air. Also caused by too much water, too much or too little light and by cold draughts.

3. The four houseplants have problems caused by not looking after them properly. For each plant, work out what you would have to do to make it healthy again. Write this down in the "Cure" column of your table.

UPPER LEAVES YELLOW

Too much calcium in the soil. May be due to watering with hard water.

4. Now write a list of things you should do with any plant to make sure it never has **any** of these problems.

WILTING LEAVES

Caused by soil being dry. Also happens if it is hot or the air is dry.

SUDDEN LEAF FALL

Caused by sudden change in temperature or level of light.

5. When you buy a houseplant, there is usually information on a label which tells you how to look after it. Labels from three different plants are shown on the left. Which plant would you put:

(a) in a bedroom?
(b) in the corner of a lounge?
(c) on a kitchen window-sill?

Explain your choices.

6. Plants make their own food by a process called PHOTOSYNTHESIS. One of the ingredients they need to do this is carbon dioxide. What two other things do the labels suggest plants need to make their food?

29

15

KEEP OUT THE KILLER

WHAT IS RABIES?

Rabies is a disease caused by a virus. All mammals can catch it—including humans. It attacks the nervous system and the victim becomes paralysed. Victims usually die.

Pet animals sometimes catch the disease if they are bitten by wild animals. If anyone is then bitten by this pet, they will also catch the disease.

Because Britain is an island it has been possible to keep rabies out. One of the main ways to keep it out is to put any animals brought into the country into quarantine for six months. This means keeping them away from all people and animals.

1. What kind of organism causes rabies?

2. What effect does this organism have on people who catch it?

3. How are people most likely to catch rabies?

BUT WHAT WOULD WE DO IF RABIES DID GET INTO BRITAIN?

Here is an account of an incident which happened in Canada. What can we learn from this?

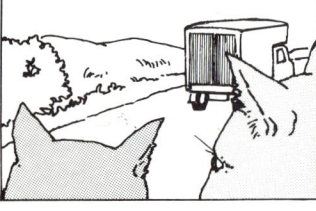

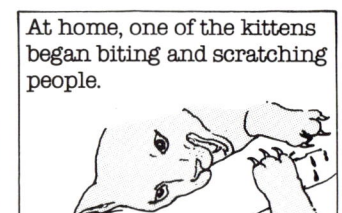

| A farmer moved away from his farm, leaving his cats behind. | Some kittens were left in a barn to fend for themselves. | A group of children walked through the farm and the kittens followed them home. | At home, one of the kittens began biting and scratching people. |

| When the kitten was examined by a vet it was found to have rabies. | Doctors checked everyone living in the area who had been in contact with the kitten to find out if they had caught rabies. | Vets had to find all the animals that might have been infected. | The problem then was to find out how the kitten became infected. One vet thought it had been bitten by a fox that had rabies. | A researcher thought the kitten might have eaten meat from an animal which had died of rabies. |

4. How is rabies most likely to get into this country?

5. Many law-abiding holiday-makers could bring rabies into the country without meaning to. Can you think of any way this could happen?

The penalties for smuggling

The most likely way that rabies could enter Britain is by people smuggling animals into the country without proper quarantine.

In 1974 a law was passed to make sure that anyone who brings an animal into Britain without putting it through quarantine will be punished. The punishments are up to a year in prison and unlimited fines. In a recent case someone let his dog off his boat while it was in harbour and was fined £1000.

Imagine you are a Public Health Inspector. Here is a typical rabies incident for you to deal with.

A family went on a camping holiday in France. They smuggled a cat with rabies into this country. The cat then bit a child. Nobody knows if the cat has scratched or bitten anybody else here, or if it has bitten any other animals. Your job is to make sure that rabies does not spread to anybody else or to any other animals.

Answer these questions to draw up a plan of action to carry out your job.

6. Explain how you would:

    (a) inform people in the area that a cat with rabies has been found.
    (b) find out if anybody else in the same street as the child has been bitten.
    (c) find out if anybody else in the whole area has been bitten.
    (d) find out if any other pets in the area have caught rabies.

7. How would you check that no wild animals living in the area (eg foxes, mice, hedgehogs or rats) have been infected with rabies?

8. What do you think should be done with any pets or wild animals which are found to have caught rabies?

9. People who take their pets abroad have to leave them in quarantine for six months when they return. How could you get the message across to people that they should not take their pets abroad unless they are willing to leave them in quarantine for six months?

16

GOODIES AND BADDIES

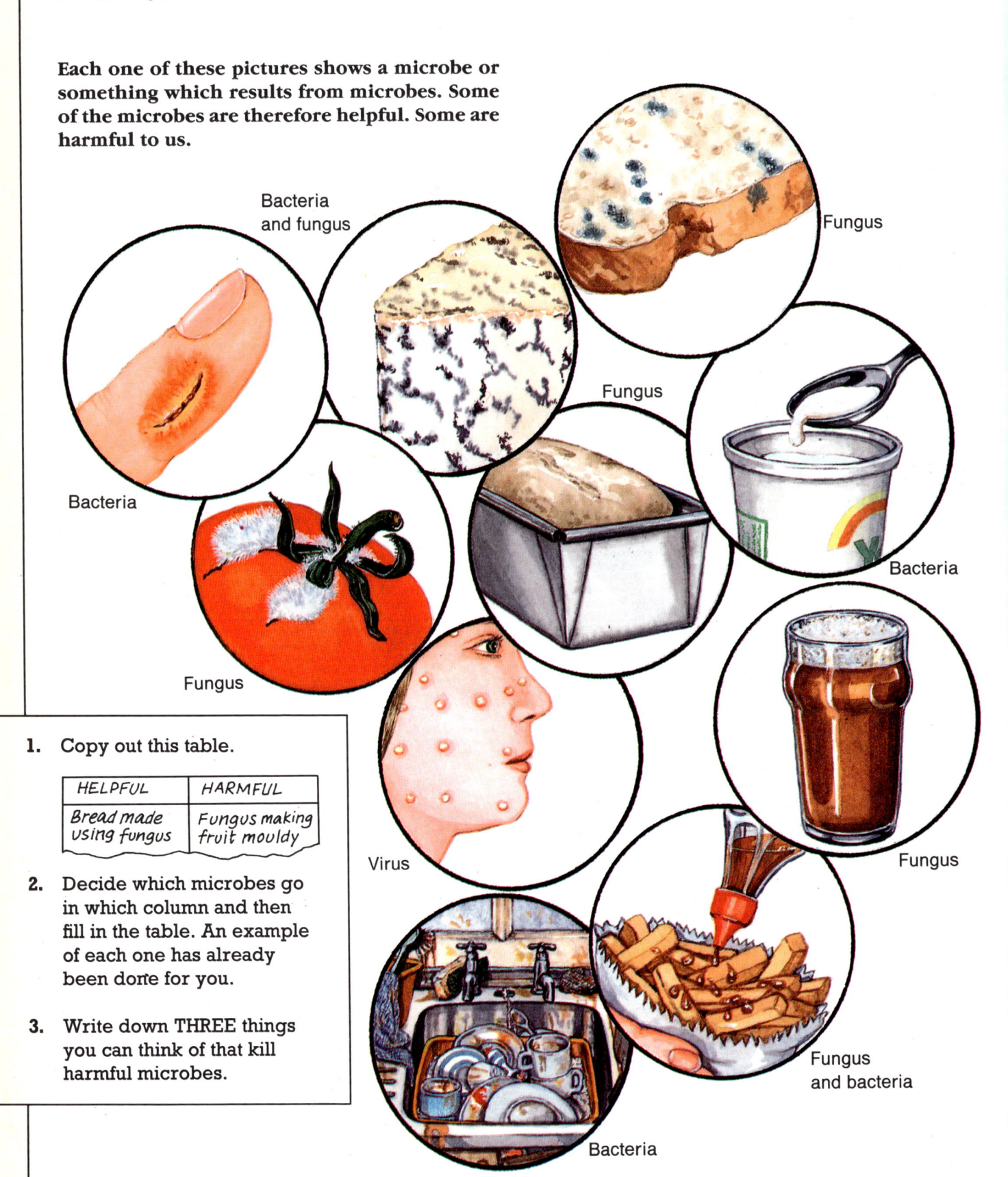

Each one of these pictures shows a microbe or something which results from microbes. Some of the microbes are therefore helpful. Some are harmful to us.

Bacteria

Bacteria and fungus

Fungus

Fungus

Bacteria

Fungus

Fungus

Virus

Bacteria

Fungus and bacteria

1. Copy out this table.

HELPFUL	HARMFUL
Bread made using fungus	Fungus making fruit mouldy

2. Decide which microbes go in which column and then fill in the table. An example of each one has already been done for you.

3. Write down THREE things you can think of that kill harmful microbes.

32

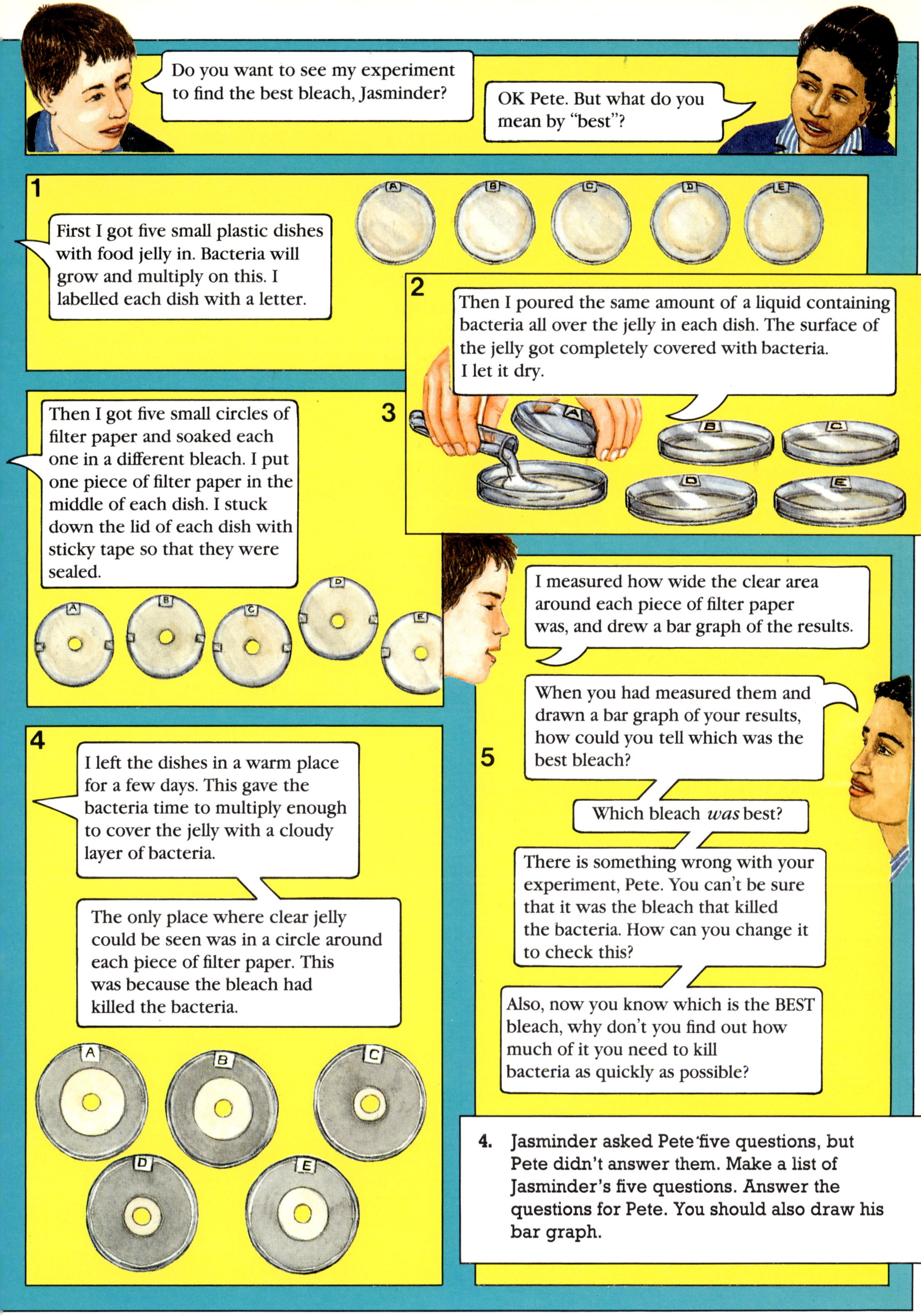

Do you want to see my experiment to find the best bleach, Jasminder?

OK Pete. But what do you mean by "best"?

1 First I got five small plastic dishes with food jelly in. Bacteria will grow and multiply on this. I labelled each dish with a letter.

2 Then I poured the same amount of a liquid containing bacteria all over the jelly in each dish. The surface of the jelly got completely covered with bacteria. I let it dry.

3 Then I got five small circles of filter paper and soaked each one in a different bleach. I put one piece of filter paper in the middle of each dish. I stuck down the lid of each dish with sticky tape so that they were sealed.

I measured how wide the clear area around each piece of filter paper was, and drew a bar graph of the results.

When you had measured them and drawn a bar graph of your results, how could you tell which was the best bleach?

4 I left the dishes in a warm place for a few days. This gave the bacteria time to multiply enough to cover the jelly with a cloudy layer of bacteria.

5 Which bleach *was* best?

There is something wrong with your experiment, Pete. You can't be sure that it was the bleach that killed the bacteria. How can you change it to check this?

The only place where clear jelly could be seen was in a circle around each piece of filter paper. This was because the bleach had killed the bacteria.

Also, now you know which is the BEST bleach, why don't you find out how much of it you need to kill bacteria as quickly as possible?

4. Jasminder asked Pete five questions, but Pete didn't answer them. Make a list of Jasminder's five questions. Answer the questions for Pete. You should also draw his bar graph.

33

17
IT'S JUST A PHASE

Adolescence is a special time in our lives. We change both physically and emotionally from being a child to becoming a young adult.

The time when physical changes take place is called puberty. The changes are caused by sex hormones. Hormones are special chemicals released by our bodies.

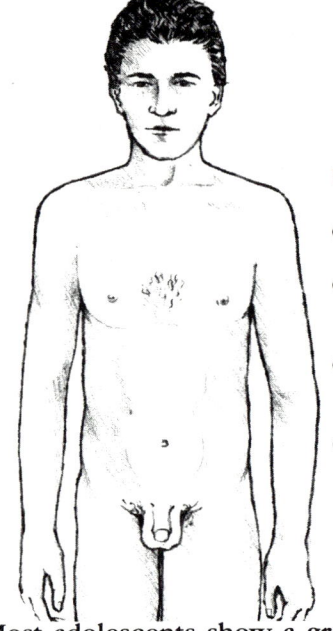

MARTIN

- growth of pubic hair
- penis and testes increase in size
- testes begin to produce sperm cells
- voice breaks and becomes deeper

JASMIN

- growth of pubic hair
- breasts develop
- hips become wider
- the ovaries start to release egg cells once a month.
- monthly periods begin
- once these changes have happened, a girl is capable of having a baby

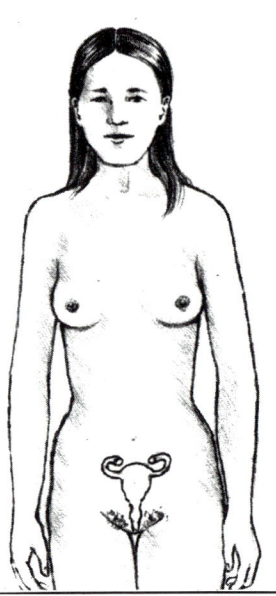

Most adolescents show a growth spurt during puberty. They rapidly increase in size and weight. This table shows the average height in centimetres of Jasmin and Martin from birth to 18 years.

AGE	0	2	4	6	8	10	12	14	16	18
Jasmin (cm)	51	88	104	117	129	140	153	161	163	163
Martin (cm)	52	88	104	117	131	141	151	164	173	175

This graph shows the proportion of boys and girls reaching puberty at different ages.

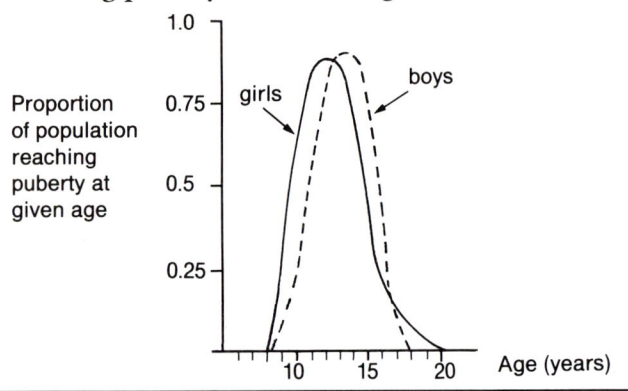

1. Draw two growth curves, one for Jasmin and one for Martin. Put both curves on the same graph.

2. In what ways are the curves similar?

3. Estimate the ages at which Jasmin and Martin began their growth spurts.

4. Do you think that adolescence always ends when the growth spurt ends? Explain your answer.

5. What is the range of ages over which

    (a) girls

    (b) boys

    reach puberty?

6. At what age do the largest number of

    (a) girls

    (b) boys

    reach puberty?

7. In 1900, the average age of a girl reaching puberty was 15. Suggest a reason for the difference between the figure for 1900 and the figure for today.

Many other changes occur during adolescence. For example, many teenagers get acne, which is an infection of the sebaceous glands in the skin. Once again, this is caused indirectly by high levels of sex hormones—acne is **not** a sign of dirtiness. It usually disappears once adolescence is over.

There are emotional changes too. Adolescents may worry about the changes that take place. The hormones themselves may affect how people feel, causing changes in mood. Many adolescents want to be independent—to make their own decisions and to question those adults who up to that time have controlled their lives. Perhaps the biggest emotional stress comes from new feelings about the opposite sex. Young people may begin to worry about what they look like and how they behave.

A. Both my best friends have started their periods but I haven't. I am really worried about this. Is there something wrong with me?
Yours a very worried 13 year old girl

B. I have suddenly become the tallest person in my class. I have grown 14 cm in 6 months! Am I going to be a giant?
Yours 12 year old girl

C. Can you explain to me why I have just started to get spots on my face and greasy skin—please!
Yours Irritated 13 yr old boy

D. My parents and I always seem to be arguing. We argue about going out, what I should wear, how I look, who I go out with etc. etc. Why has this just started happening?
Yours Concerned 15 year old girl

E. I used to be very good friends with the girl next door. All of a sudden I feel really shy when I am with her and it is awkward when we are together. Why have I just started to feel like this?
Yours, 12 yr old boy

8. Read the letters **A** to **E**. For each one, write down a piece of scientific information which would help the writers to understand their problems.

Some people think that adolescence ends when a young person becomes a 'responsible adult'—but what does this mean?

9. Suggest THREE examples for each of the following

   (a) Behaviour which you think is irresponsible.

   (b) Behaviour which adults think is irresponsible but which you think is acceptable.

10. Explain why adolescents need to have a responsible sexual attitude even before adolescence ends.

18
MESSAGE ON A BOTTLE

1. What do you think the bumps on the surfaces of the bottles are for?

2. The bumps carry a message. The message is the same on every bottle. What do you think it says?

3. What could be done to make sure that **all** bottles which need the message on actually carry it?

A few years ago, the Royal National Institute for the Blind, the Government, and manufacturers of dangerous chemicals got together. They wanted to work out a system of marking plastic bottles. The system was to be used to warn visually handicapped people that there was a dangerous chemical inside.

Unfortunately they couldn't agree on a useful message, so there is still no standard way of marking bottles. Some manufacturers went ahead and put messages on their bottles. They used one of the two alphabets which some visually handicapped people can read using their sense of touch. The two alphabets are called BRAILLE and MOON.

4. Here is a message which often appears on bottles, written in the Moon alphabet.

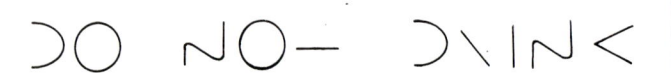

⊃O NO— ⊃\l∩<

Use the key to the Moon alphabet on the right to work out what this message says.

5. Write out a message of your own to put on bottles which contain flammable chemicals. Use the Moon alphabet again.

THE MOON ALPHABET

A	B	C	D	E	F
∧	⊂	C	⊃	⌐	⌂

G	H	I	J	K	L
⌒	O	|	J	<	L

M	N	O	P	Q	R
⊓	N	O	∠	⌐	\

S	T	U	V	W	X
/	—	U	V	∩	>

Y	Z
⌐	⌐

THE BRAILLE ALPHABET

A B
C D
E F
G H
I J
K L
M N
O P
Q R
S T
U V
W X
Y Z

6. Name five different chemicals you have in your home which you think are dangerous.

7. If you were visually handicapped, what message would you want printed on the bottle of each of these dangerous chemicals?

8. Write out this message using the Braille alphabet.

9. Most visually handicapped people cannot read Braille or Moon. This means that other ways have to be used to warn them that a bottle contains a dangerous chemical. It is useful to know that most visually handicapped people have **some** vision. Write a list of changes you could make to the design of a normal bottle to warn visually handicapped people.

10. Use some of the ideas in your list for question 9 to design a bottle to hold a dangerous chemical.

Royal National Institute for the Blind
224 Great Portland Street, London W1N 6AA

RNIB

Designing buildings for visually handicapped people

LIGHT   COLOUR   TEXTURE   SOUND

11. This booklet tells people what they can do to improve the design of homes for visually handicapped people. What four words appear on the cover to give ideas for designing household objects?

12. Write a list of changes you could make to your living room at home so that a visually handicapped person could find things in it. Use the four words from question 11 to help you.

19
IT'S ALL IN THE GENES

In the nineteenth century a monk called Gregor Mendel carried out experiments to find out how features are passed from parents to their offspring. He thought that children looked like their parents because something is passed from parents to children when the egg from the mother is fertilised by the sperm from the father.

The Daily Blurb *has arranged an exclusive interview with Gregor Mendel...*

Gregor Mendel

Reporter: Thank you for giving me an interview, Father Gregor. I understand you used pea plants in your experiments. Why did you choose pea plants?

Mendel: I chose pea plants because they are easy to grow and observe. Also, there are a number of different types which I could cross with one another. For example, tall and dwarf types.

TALL Crossed with... DWARF

Mendel: I crossed tall plants with dwarf plants. I collected all the seeds from these parent plants and planted them. All the seeds grew into tall plants.

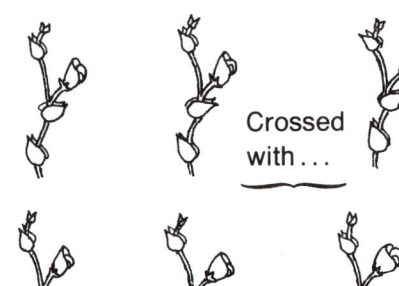

ALL TALL OFFSPRING OR "CHILDREN"

Crossed with...

Mendel: Then I crossed these tall offspring. Again I collected all the seeds and planted them.

Mendel: This time tall *and* dwarf plants grew. There were three tall plants for every one dwarf plant.

THREE TALL FOR EVERY ONE DWARF OFFSPRING OR "GRANDCHILDREN"

Reporter: What did you conclude from these results?

Mendel: I concluded that parents pass something on to their offspring which often makes them look like their parents. Whatever it is that is passed on, the offspring can pass it on to *their* offspring. In this way, features of one generation can be passed down to children, grandchildren, and so on.

Mendel: This discovery is very important. For example, it means that we will be able to improve the plants and animals we grow for food so that they grow bigger more quickly. All we have to do now is to find out exactly what is passed from parents to offspring.

1. Scientists have now found that it is **genes** which are passed from parents to offspring. Imagine that you are the reporter on the *Daily Blurb*. Write an article for your newspaper about Mendel's work. Use these guidelines to help you:

    (a) Think of a catchy headline.
    (b) Write short sentences and short paragraphs.
    (c) Use pictures to illustrate the article.
    (d) Have one or two quotes from Mendel in the article.
    (e) Explain where genes fit into the story.
    (f) Explain what benefit Mendel thought this knowledge would give.

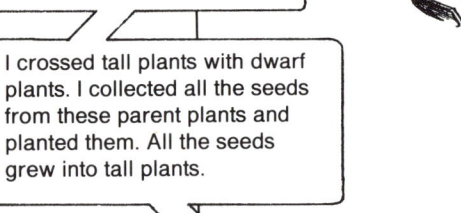

Can you roll your tongue like this?

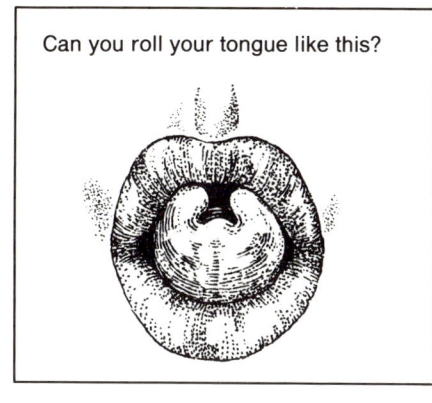

Do you have ear lobes... or no ear lobes?

Are your eyes brown, or blue, or green, or some other colour?

Many people are very similar to other members of their family. Differences between people are called VARIATION.

HAPPY FAMILIES

COUPLE A   COUPLE B   COUPLE C

Julie   Paul   Gary   Chris
Surinder   Rajwant   Sara   Selena

2. Have a go at "Happy Families". Write down the names of the children that you think belong to each of the couples.

3. Explain how you could guess which children go with which parents.

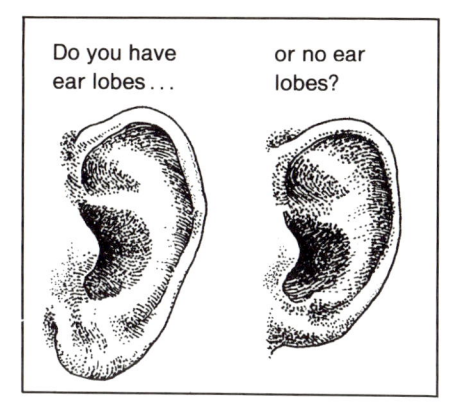

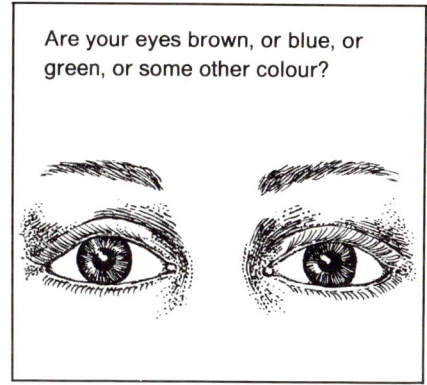

Can you do this... ...or this?

4. What is unusual about the hand on the right?

5. Try to explain how a person with a hand like this would come to have this unusual feature. Use the word "genes" in your answer.

Someone with a hand like the one on the right would not find it a problem in daily life. Unfortunately, some people have unusual genes which cause diseases passed on to them. Some of the diseases may even kill the people who have them.

One disease caused by unusual genes passed from parents to children is **sickle-cell anaemia** (pronounced an-eem-ee-a). It affects the red blood cells which carry oxygen around the body. People with this disease are very weak and often die when they are young.

Sickle-cell anaemia red blood cell

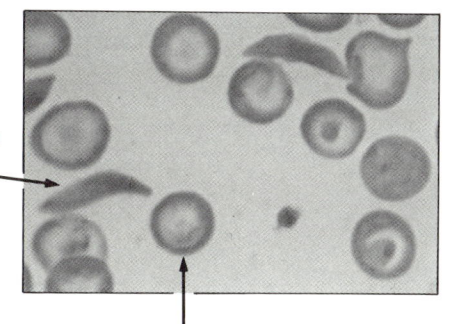

Normal red blood cell

6. Describe how sickle-cell anaemia blood differs from normal blood.

7. Why would somebody with these unusual cells be very weak?

20
A TALE OF THE RIVER BED

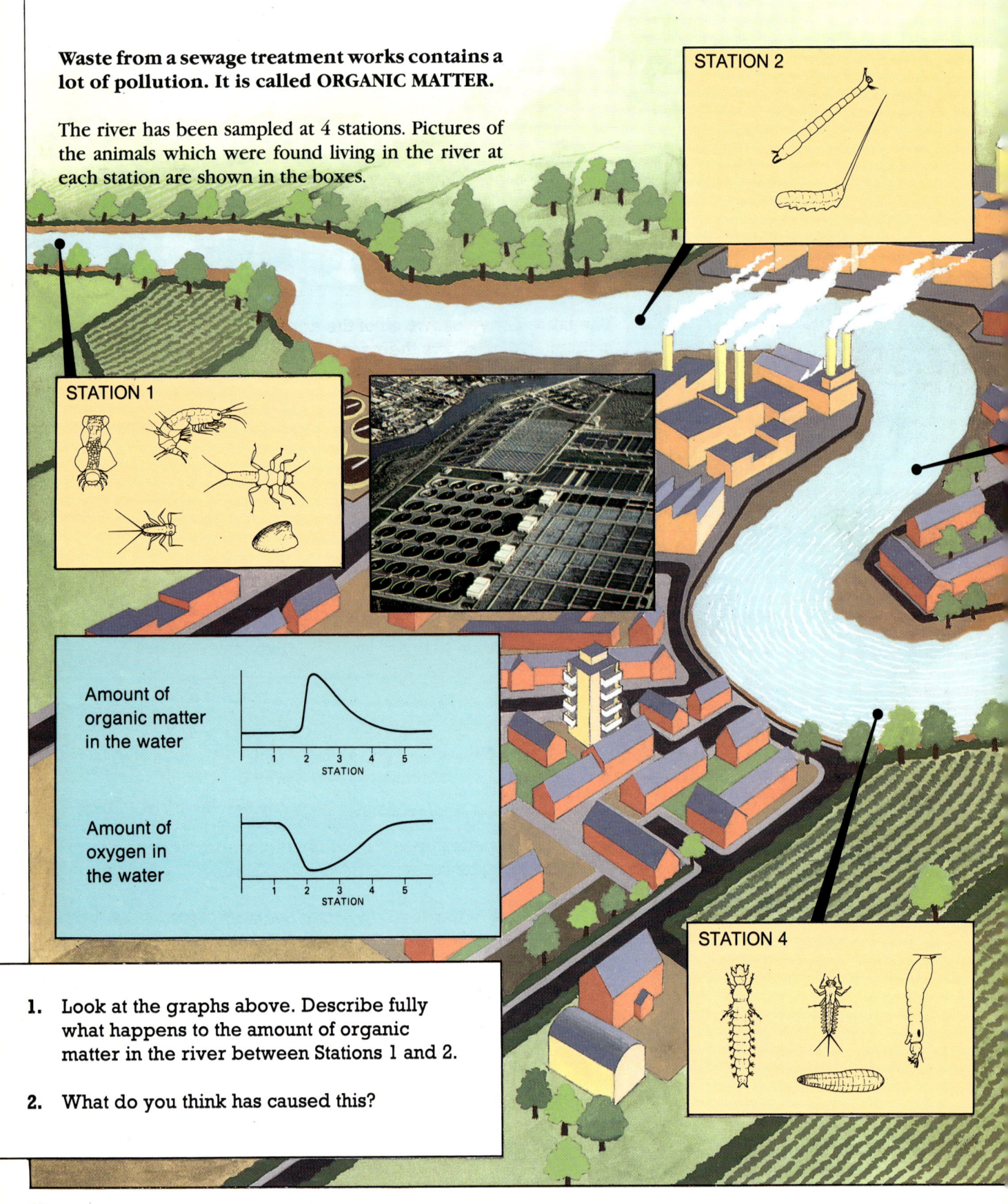

Waste from a sewage treatment works contains a lot of pollution. It is called ORGANIC MATTER.

The river has been sampled at 4 stations. Pictures of the animals which were found living in the river at each station are shown in the boxes.

STATION 2

STATION 1

Amount of organic matter in the water

Amount of oxygen in the water

STATION 4

1. Look at the graphs above. Describe fully what happens to the amount of organic matter in the river between Stations 1 and 2.

2. What do you think has caused this?

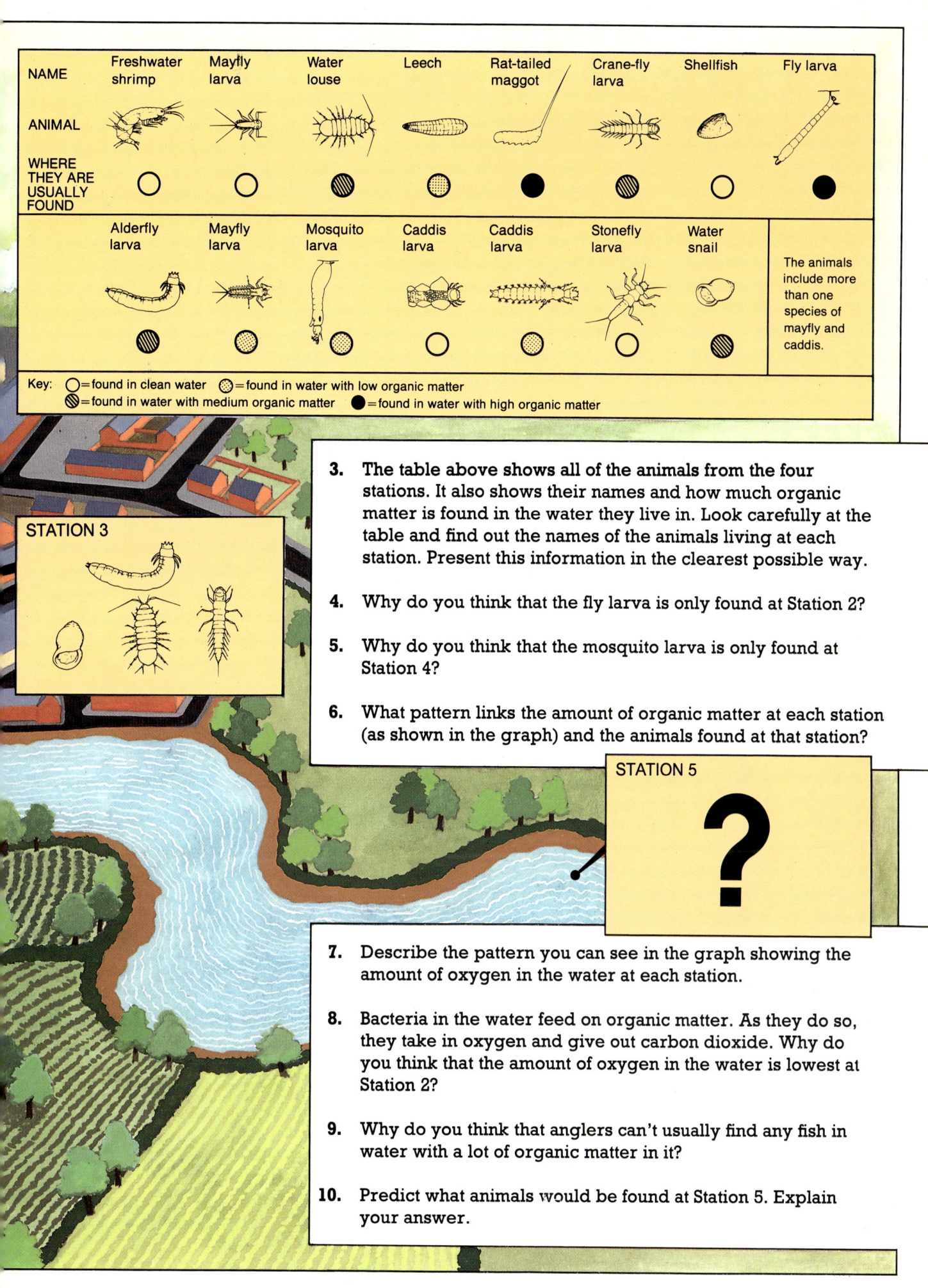

NAME	Freshwater shrimp	Mayfly larva	Water louse	Leech	Rat-tailed maggot	Crane-fly larva	Shellfish	Fly larva
ANIMAL								
WHERE THEY ARE USUALLY FOUND	○	○	◍	◌	●	◍	○	●

NAME	Alderfly larva	Mayfly larva	Mosquito larva	Caddis larva	Caddis larva	Stonefly larva	Water snail	
ANIMAL								The animals include more than one species of mayfly and caddis.
WHERE THEY ARE USUALLY FOUND	◍	◌	◌	○	◌	○	◍	

Key: ○ = found in clean water   ◌ = found in water with low organic matter
◍ = found in water with medium organic matter   ● = found in water with high organic matter

STATION 3

3. The table above shows all of the animals from the four stations. It also shows their names and how much organic matter is found in the water they live in. Look carefully at the table and find out the names of the animals living at each station. Present this information in the clearest possible way.

4. Why do you think that the fly larva is only found at Station 2?

5. Why do you think that the mosquito larva is only found at Station 4?

6. What pattern links the amount of organic matter at each station (as shown in the graph) and the animals found at that station?

STATION 5
?

7. Describe the pattern you can see in the graph showing the amount of oxygen in the water at each station.

8. Bacteria in the water feed on organic matter. As they do so, they take in oxygen and give out carbon dioxide. Why do you think that the amount of oxygen in the water is lowest at Station 2?

9. Why do you think that anglers can't usually find any fish in water with a lot of organic matter in it?

10. Predict what animals would be found at Station 5. Explain your answer.

Matrix of the Relationship between Activities and Attainment Targets of the National Curriculum

	1 The Good, The Bad and The Ugly	2 What makes a Weed successful?	3 Spotting the Difference	4 On the Beach	5 Super Human!	6 S-Factors	7 Having Children	8 The Right Choice	9 Mouth Matters	10 Confined to the Cell	11 Coronary Heart Disease	12 Aerobics	13 Grow Your Own	14 Unhappy Houseplants	15 Keep out the Killer	16 Goodies and Baddies	17 It's Just a Phase	18 Message on a Bottle	19 It's all in the Genes	20 A Tale of the River Bed
1 Exploration of science	✓	✓				✓					✓				✓	✓				
2 The variety of life	✓	✓	✓																	
3 Processes of life				✓	✓	✓	✓	✓	✓	✓	✓	✓	✓	✓	✓	✓				
4 Genetics and Evolution							✓											✓		
5 Human influences on the Earth											✓								✓	
7 Making new materials												✓								

INDEX

Numbers refer to units, not pages.

adaptation   1
adolescence   17
aerobics   12
aerobic respiration   12
algae   4
anaerobic respiration   12
arthropods   4

bacteria   10
behaviour   3
bladder   5
blood vessels   5, 11
bones   5
braille   18
brain   5
bypass operation   11

carbohydrate   8
cells, human   7, 10
cells, plant   10
chlorophyll   13
chloroplast   10
classification   4
coelenterates   4
competition   2
conception   7
coronary artery   11
coronary heart disease   11
cytoplasm   10

diet   8

echinoderms   4
exercise   6
experimental design   2, 3

fat   8
ferns   4
fibre   8
fishes   4
fitness   6
flowering plants   4
food groups   8
food poisoning   10
fuel burning   13

genes   7, 19
greenhouses   13
groups of living things   4

habitat   1, 4
heart   5, 11
heart attack   11
hormones, sex   17
human body   5

inheritance   19
inherited diseases   19

kidneys   5

lungs   5

mammals   4
Mendel   19
microbes   16
minerals   8
molluscs   4
moon alphabet   18
mosses   4
muscles   5

nerves   5

observable features   4
organ systems   5, 6
organ transplants   5

photosynthesis   10, 13, 14
plant growth   14
pregnancy   7
protein   8
puberty   17

rabies   15
reproduction   7
reproductive organs   7
respiration   10, 12
robots   5

salmonella   10
sickle-cell anaemia   19
skin   5
smoking   11
speed of reactions   6
sperm   7
stamina   6
starch   13
stomach   5
strength   6
suppleness   6

teeth   9
tongue rolling   19
tooth decay   9

variation   19
virus   15
visually handicapped   18
vitamins   8

water pollution   20
weeds   2
woodlice   3

43

Acknowledgements

The publishers would like to thank the following for supplying photographs for these units:

1 Mary Evans Picture Library
9 The British Dental Health Foundation
10 Science Photo Library
18 The Royal National Institute for the Blind
19 The Department of Medical Illustration, St Bartholomew's Hospital (Sickle-cell anaemia blood); Ann Ronan Picture Library (Gregor Mendel)
20 The Water Authorities Association

Back cover: Biofotos/Andrew Henley